TRUE CHAMPIONS PURSUE GREATNESS
IN ALL AREAS OF LIFE

EXCELLENCE

CHAD BONHAM, GENERAL EDITOR

**FELLOWSHIP OF
CHRISTIAN ATHLETES**

THE HEART AND SOUL IN SPORTS

Regal

From Gospel Light
Ventura, California, U.S.A.

Published by Regal
From Gospel Light
Ventura, California, U.S.A.
www.regalbooks.com
Printed in the U.S.A.

Library of Congress Cataloging-in-Publication Data
Excellence.
p. cm.
"Fellowship of Christian Athletes."
ISBN 978-0-8307-4629-3 (trade paper)
1. Athletes—Religious life. 2. Excellence—Religious aspects—Christianity. I.
Fellowship of Christian Athletes.
BV4596.A8E95 2009
248.8′8—dc22
2008043536

1 2 3 4 5 6 7 8 9 10 / 16 15 14 13 12 11 10 09

Rights for publishing this book outside the U.S.A. or in non-English
languages are administered by Gospel Light Worldwide, an international
not-for-profit ministry. For additional information, please visit www.glww.org,
email info@glww.org, or write to Gospel Light Worldwide,
1957 Eastman Avenue, Ventura, CA 93003, U.S.A.

CONTENTS

THE FOUR CORE

Dan Britton

Senior Vice President of Ministries, Fellowship of Christian Athletes

The NCAA Final Four tournament is an exciting sporting event. Even if you are not a person who likes basketball, it is awesome to watch March Madness as it narrows down 64 teams into 4 core teams. This makes me think about Fellowship of Christian Athlete's "Four Core"—not four core teams, but four core values.

Core values are simply the way you live and conduct yourself. They are your attitudes, beliefs and convictions. Values should be what you are, not what you want to become. The goal is to embody your values every step of the way.

Are your values just words, or do you actually live them out? Can others identify the values in your life without your telling them? Your values need to be a driving force that shapes the way you do life! Talk is cheap, but values are valuable.

When everything is stripped away, what is left? For FCA, it is integrity, serving, teamwork and excellence. These Four Core are so powerful to me that I have made them my own personal values. So, I have to ask you, what are your values? What guides you? Let me share with you FCA's Four Core, which are even better than the Final Four!

Integrity

To have integrity means that you are committed to Christlike wholeness, both privately and publicly. Basically, it means to live without gaps. Proverbs 11:3 says that integrity should guide you, but that a double life will destroy you. You need to be transparent, authentic, honest and trustworthy. You should be the same in all situations and not become someone different when the competition of the game begins. Integrity means to act the same when no one is looking. It is not about being perfect, but, as a coach or athlete, you need to be the real deal.

Serving

In John 13:12-15, Jesus gives us the perfect example of serving when He washes the disciples' feet. He then commands the disciples to go and do unto others what He has done to them. How many of your teammates' feet have you washed? Maybe not literally, but spiritually, do you have an attitude of serving just as if you were washing their feet in the locker room? You need to seek out the needs of others and be passionate about pursuing people who are needy. And, the last time I checked, everyone is needy.

Teamwork

Teamwork means to work together with others and express unity in Christ in all of your relationships. In Philippians 2:1-5, Paul encourages each of us to be one, united together in spirit and purpose. We all need to be on one team—not just the team we play on, but on God's Team! We need to equip, encourage and empower one another. Do you celebrate and hurt together as teammates? You need to be arm-in-arm with others, locking up together to accomplish God's work. There should be no Lone Rangers.

Excellence

To pursue excellence means to honor and glorify God in everything you do. In Colossians 3:23-24, Paul writes, "whatever you do, work at it with all your heart, as working for the Lord, not for men." The "whatever" part is hard, because it means that everything you do must be done for God, not others. You need to pursue excellence in practice, in games, in schoolwork and in lifting weights. God deserves your best, not your leftovers.

It is tip-off time for the game of life. How will you be known?

Whatever happens, conduct yourselves in a manner worthy of the gospel of Christ.
PHILIPPIANS 1:27, *NIV*

Lord Jesus, my prayer is to live and compete with integrity, serving, teamwork and excellence. It is a high standard, but I know that with Your power and strength, it can happen. I want all my relationships to be known for things that are of You. Search my heart and reveal to me my values. I lay at the foot of the cross the values that do not honor You, and I ask for Your forgiveness. The values that bring You glory, I lay them at the foot of the cross for Your anointing.

LEAVE A MARK

I have been crucified with Christ and I no longer live, but Christ lives in me. The life I live in the body, I live by faith in the Son of God, who loved me and gave himself for me.

GALATIANS 2:20, *NIV*

An imprint is a permanent mark. To make an imprint means to engrave, etch, impress or inscribe. When I was eight years old, I had a once-in-a-lifetime opportunity to ride my older brother's motorcycle. Wanting to show him how big and tough I was, I took off at full speed! Less than 100 yards down the dirt road, the cycle's front tire hit a hole, which sent me flying! I landed in a nearby ditch, and the motorcycle landed on my back. Talk about painful!

Fortunately, the curve of the ditch allowed most of my body to be spared from the impact. The only part of the motorcycle that was touching me was the muffler, which was pressing into my back. Unfortunately, since it was hot, the muffler burned through my shirt and my flesh, and I experienced a new level of pain. My brother came quickly to my rescue, which spared me from being seriously wounded. I was, however, banned from riding his bike ever again. And even though the wreck happened 33 years ago, I still have a nice burn mark on my back—the imprint of that hot muffler.

Think about this: Every time we compete, coach or lead, we leave an imprint. Whether it is a positive or a negative impression is up to us. When we are committed to excellence, we naturally desire to leave the kind of mark on others that will have an eternal impact. As a part of this commitment, we all, as followers of Christ, need to be intentional in striving, straining and stretching to give our very best in all areas.

When I was younger, I was shown what it meant to leave an imprint of excellence. My grandfather, "Pop," showed me what it meant to pursue excellence by staying spiritually hungry. One month before he died, I went to visit Pop at his home. As we talked in his living room, I noticed three items he kept on his end table: a large-print Bible, a magnifying glass and a tape recorder.

I knew that his eyesight had been failing for years, which accounted for the first two things, but the tape recorder puzzled me. Out of curiosity, I asked him about it. His answer astonished me. "This is where I meet God every morning," he said, "and unfortunately by the end of the day, I sometimes forget what He taught me from His Word. I decided that if I read the Bible *and* listened to it on tape, I'd double my chance of remembering it." My grandfather was spiritually hungry and was willing to do whatever it took to feed that desire. He was pursuing excellence to the very end.

When it comes to the pursuit of excellence, the ultimate question is not whether we leave a good or bad imprint but whether we leave an imprint of ourselves or of Jesus. What a challenge! My grandfather certainly left an imprint of Christ on me, and I must continually ask myself if I am doing the same for others.

Whether we are playing or coaching or leading, we all must be committed to excellence and to leaving behind the imprint of Christ. What about you? Do you pursue excellence? Are you marking others with excellence? Give the Lord what's right, not what's left. Leave a mark—or, better yet, leave an imprint of Jesus. That is a true reflection of a commitment to excellence.

How to Use This Book

Excellence takes an in-depth look at this core value and comes at it from 12 different angles as lived out by 12 different people. Their insights shed new light on this value and give us a model to follow.

You can read *Excellence* individually or as part of a group. As part of a personal devotion time, you can gain insight as you read through each story and ponder on the "Training Time" questions at the end. Mentors can also use this book in a discipleship relationship, using the "Training Time" questions to step up to the next level. And small groups (huddles) can study the core value as a group to be prepared to sharpen each other with questions.

The Big Win

Tony Dungy

Winning Super Bowl Coach of the Indianapolis Colts

Do you not know that the runners in a stadium all race, but only one receives the prize? Run in such a way that you may win.

1 CORINTHIANS 9:24

For when the One Great Scorer comes to write against your name, He marks—not that you won or lost—but how you played the Game.

GRANTLAND RICE, "ALUMNUS FOOTBALL"

From the Pee Wee Leagues to the professional ranks, there is one constant truth when it comes to coaching: Practice makes perfect.

No better example of this time-tested principle can be found than with Indianapolis Colts' head coach Tony Dungy. Known for practicing what he preaches (although saying the soft-spoken leader preaches would be somewhat of a stretch), Dungy has taken his disciplined methods beyond the football field and into his personal life. That's why he is such a strong proponent of the Fellowship of Christian Athletes' four core values.

"If you just practice one day a week, you're never going to be as good as if you practice every day," Dungy says. "And that's what it's all about, really. It's reading and understanding what God wants you to do and then putting it into practice. When you come up a little short and don't quite get it, don't give up. Continue to work at it. Say, 'Okay, Lord, I fell a little bit short in this area. Give me another opportunity so that I can continue to work on it.' The more you practice those values, the easier they become, and the better you get at them."

Of those four core values, Dungy has especially been equated with excellence throughout his coaching career. It's a characteristic that has shone brightly during his greatest victory (the Super Bowl XLI in 2007) and his greatest tragedy (the passing of his oldest son, James, in 2005).

Colt linebacker Tyjuan Hagler—who has played for Dungy since 2005—is one of the many eyewitnesses to that fact. "I've learned a lot about how strong his faith is," Hagler says. "When the tragedy occurred, we went down [to Tampa] for the funeral. When we were waiting, we were seated in this room; and when he walked through the door, he had the biggest smile on his face. I was just thinking, *He's got the biggest smile on his face, and he is just hurting so bad inside.* That really touched me."

Hagler likewise experienced Super Bowl bliss with the Colts in February 2007 and can honestly attest to Dungy's even-keeled approach to excellence. "He's the same guy," says Hagler. "When we won the championship, he praised

God. He gave the honor to Christ, and he said that without Christ, none of us would be here right now. He did the same thing when he lost his son that he did when we won the Super Bowl. He put both situations in God's hands."

FCA president and CEO Les Steckel has likewise observed Dungy over the years and got a firsthand look at Dungy's quest for excellence. (Steckel was the offensive coordinator for the Tampa Bay Buccaneers in 2000 when Dungy served as that team's head from 1996 to 2000). "One thing that people don't understand about coaching in the NFL is the tremendous pressures," Steckel says. "Tony Dungy taught me a great deal about handling those. Under all the pressure, I knew that his stomach was turning, but his demeanor was awesome. That countenance that he continues to display to this day was one that we all wish we had in pressure-packed times in our lives."

According to Kansas City Chiefs' head coach Herman Edwards—who was an assistant coach at Tampa Bay from 1996 to 2000—Dungy also displayed excellence by readily taking responsibility for the team's failures. "Anytime we had a bad day on defense, people would ask him what happened, and he'd just say, 'Well, we just have to tackle a little bit better,'" Edwards recalls. "He never ran down the players out there. He would just say that we needed to coach them a little better, and at the end of the day, he was right. That's what we needed to do better."

Tampa Bay cornerback Ronde Barber, who played for Dungy from 1996 to 2000, uncovered another aspect of the excellence Dungy strives for: patience. This component of Dungy's character is spoken of in Proverbs 19:11, which states, "A man's wisdom gives him patience; it is to his glory to overlook an offense." "Not everything is solved with haste and urgency," Barber agrees. "You can be urgent and patient at the same time. Tony was always good at keeping everything in perspective."

Perhaps the most astute observation of Dungy has come from running back Shaun Alexander, who clearly recognizes the role that one's purpose in life plays in relation to excellence. "[Dungy] accepts the calling he has been given," Alexander says. "He is called to glorify God and be a champion. He walks it, talks it, lives it. You see it in his eyes. He will compete and fight until the end, all the while smiling at his opponents."

Dungy's definition of excellence, on the other hand, is a bit more straightforward and, true to coaching form, textbook in nature. "Excellence is doing something at the very highest level it can be done using all your capabilities and everything God has given you," says Dungy. "Sometimes that gets lost. We don't always think of excellence as a Christian concept, but I think God does desire us to be excellent at what we do."

Dungy can think of many examples of excellence in athletics, such as legendary head coach Chuck Noll, for whom he played at Pittsburgh from 1977 to 1978. But in his mind, no one can surpass the level of excellence that his parents, Wilbur and CleoMae Dungy, modeled for him

15

growing up in Jackson, Michigan. "My parents were definitions of excellence in teaching," Dungy says. "It was important to them to be the best that they could be—not for personal reasons, but that was their concept of serving. They wanted to serve people in the best way possible."

"I think excellence is something we have to be cognizant of," he adds. "Just because we're Christians doesn't mean we should take the approach to just move forward and let the Lord handle it. We do have a responsibility to be the very best we can be in whatever field we decide to take up."

Dungy believes that Christ-centered excellence is usually either taught incorrectly (with the emphasis being toward personal benefit as opposed to God's glory) or isn't taught at all. His first exposure to the concept came at an FCA camp where he learned about Paul's athletic reference in 1 Corinthians 9:24-27. In particular, Dungy was drawn to verse 24, which says, "Run in such a way that you may win."

"That's the first time that it hit me biblically that we aren't supposed to be satisfied with mediocrity or think that winning is the wrong goal to have," Dungy recalls. "It says run to win, but understand what the prize is and understand that we've got to compete for spiritual things and long-lasting things. There's nothing wrong with being excellent, and that verse has always stuck out to me."

One of the dangers of achieving excellence comes in the form of pride—that is, when the individual who has achieved success because of their excellence takes the credit and in turn uses it for their own personal gain. Dungy has seen this play out in the lives of many athletes and has likewise seen the shallow results.

"If you're running to win, but you have only earthly goals in mind, it will be short lived," Dungy says. "It will be a withering type of thing. You have to have those spiritual goals in mind. Things do get in the way of being excellent. Some of those things are pride and self-centeredness, but you still have to do everything as unto the Lord. You have to try to keep those types of thoughts out."

Dungy also says our purpose behind striving for excellence must always be balanced and in tune with God's plan for our lives. Otherwise, we might become like the rich man Jesus tells about in the parable He shares in Luke 12:13-21. The landowner, blessed with a bountiful crop, decides to build bigger barns for his abundance and then says that he will "take it easy" (v. 19). But the rich man is in for a rude awakening: "God said to him, 'You fool! This very night your life is demanded of you. And the things you have prepared—whose will they be?'" (v. 20).

"That's where you have to understand what's spiritual and what's long lasting," Dungy says. "Where is your soul? That's the thing that's going to last. We do get misguided priorities if we're just thinking only in terms of excellence. Everything has to balance out. Excellence without service or excellence without teamwork is excellence for only your purpose. It all has to come into balance."

For coaches and athletes, excellence is often defined in terms of wins and losses. Those who find themselves in the winner's circle are deemed excellent by virtue of their accomplishment, while those who struggle to win often have their excellence questioned.

Similar yardsticks are used in other areas of life. Business, entertainment, arts, science, fashion and most everything in popular culture are all judged by the world's standard of success, which creates a tricky road that must be carefully maneuvered—especially for believers and followers of Christ.

"You have to try to keep your priorities straight," Dungy says. "You have to look at the world from a Christian point of view, which isn't always easy to do. There are going to be times when you don't win. There are going to be times when you get fired, and you can't let that affect your self-esteem. You can't let it affect your outlook, because we have to measure ourselves by a different standard than by the world's standard."

Dungy believes that wins and losses are one of sports' great inspirations to excellence, but he also fully understands the danger that lies within that dynamic. For instance, too often society falls into the trap of demeaning and devaluing anyone who fails to reach a certain level of success. With that in mind, Dungy focuses on performance and effort more than the final result.

"We do have a scoreboard that measures the final tally of the game," he says. "But we don't all have the same opportunities. We don't all have the same talent. So to me, more than the scoreboard, I like to focus on how our team is doing. Are we doing everything we can? Are we using all of the ability that God has given us?

"There will be days for my football team when we win that I'm not happy because we didn't really play excellent, we didn't practice as well as we can, we didn't use those talents. There are other games when we lose and I have to say, 'You know what? We gave it everything we had. We did as much as we could do. It just wasn't our day today, but I'm really proud of our team.' To me, it's more about knowing what my potential is and if I live up to that day in and day out."

And for Dungy, it all comes back to how you define excellence. Is it defined by the number of games won or by individual performance? If the former is the case, disappointment is sure to follow. "But excellence is about how you do things and doing the very best you can," Dungy says. "Excellence doesn't mean you always have to win or always have to be in first place."

To maintain that healthy perspective, Dungy says the key is staying focused on Christ. "If you're only focused on excellence in your job or excellence on the field, you will get totally out of balance and out of whack. Yes, I need to be excellent as a coach. I need to be excellent as a Christian. I need to be excellent as a father. I need to be excellent as a person in the community and strive for that excellence everywhere and not just in one area."

That also means never sacrificing integrity for excellence. Although an increasing number of athletes and coaches have succumbed to the temptation to cheat, Dungy can point to another of Jesus' parables found in Matthew 7:24-27 for his inspiration to avoid such lapses in one's character. The story talks about two men—one who builds his house on the rock and the other who builds his house on the sand. When the rains came, the house built on the rock stands firm while the house built on sand crumbles to the ground.

That vivid imagery illustrates what happens to those who heed God's call to competitive integrity versus those who cut corners and look for a quick fix on their route to success. The latter cannot be legitimately equated with godly excellence.

"You have to look at excellence in every way," Dungy says. "I have to be excellent in my integrity, not just excellent in winning. If I'm just trying to be excellent in winning, that can lead to some problems. We are bound by rules, and we are not going to cheat or do certain things to win, but that is still the goal—to be excellent. And there is nothing wrong with that. As Christians, it is great to be able to show the world that, yes, we can do it the Lord's way, but we can be excellent while we do it."

And according to 1 Chronicles 4:9-10, striving for excellence can have a tangible result. Jabez, a man referred to in verse 9 as "more honorable than his brothers," unabashedly made his desire known to God. In verse 10,

Jabez says, "If only You would bless me, extend my border, let Your hand be with me, and keep me from harm, so that I will not cause any pain." That same verse concludes by telling us that "God granted his request."

While the end result may be different for each individual—based on God's purpose for his or her life—ultimately excellence can be wrapped up by what Paul wrote in 2 Timothy 4:7: "I have fought the good fight, I have finished the race, I have kept the faith" and 1 Corinthians 9:24, the Scripture that so impressed Dungy: "Do you not know that the runners in a stadium all race, but only one receives the prize? Run in such a way that you may win." Both passages allude to the "big win" that is yet to be awarded in heaven.

"I talk about excellence a lot, because I think from a Christian perspective, that can get lost sometimes," Dungy says. "We talk so much about how it's 'just God's will' and that we want to serve Him, but He wants us to be excellent in what we do. He's placed us in our careers. We all run to receive a prize and to win. I never want to forget that part of it. We should run to win."

TRAINING TIME

1. For Tony Dungy and other NFL coaches, the "big win" can be equated with a victory in the Super Bowl. What does the "big win" mean for you in your life?

2. What are some of the characteristics that Dungy's NFL peers say have contributed to his excellent results both on and off the field? How do you think your peers would describe your pursuit of excellence? What characteristics would you like to see increased in your life so that excellence would be possible?

3. Read 1 Corinthians 9:24-27. As a follower of Christ, what do you think it means to "win the prize"? What are some examples of "perishable" crowns? What is your concept of an "imperishable" crown?

4. Read Luke 12:13-21. What different types of people in modern society does the rich man in this parable represent? What are the dangers of resting, or taking it easy, after achieving varying degrees of success? What message about excellence do you think Jesus is trying to tell us through this parable?

5. Read 2 Timothy 4:1-8. What are some things Paul says we will have to endure? How does having the proper perspective on winning and losing while we are in the midst of pursuing excellence help us deal with such challenges?

"Being an excellent coach means doing everything as well as you can do it. That is everything from preparing your players to dealing with the media. Whatever is in front of me, whatever is on my plate as a coach, I want to do it as well as I can, because there is never a time when I am not to be exemplifying Christ. Whatever role I have, whether it is running simple drills behind the scenes during practice or making a decision with one minute left in the Super Bowl, I am going to do it as well as I possibly can. I think that's part of what the Lord would want us to do. It is human nature to say, 'I won't give 100 percent. I'll just give what I need to, to do my job well.' Or if I'm lifting weights, 'I could do one more repetition, but I don't want to push it.' But the Lord says, 'Do as well as you can with the gifts I've given you.' That's what I always look at. Are we doing absolutely all that we can with the talent and opportunities that God gives us? That's what excellence is. I could win every game and still not be playing excellent if I'm not really giving everything that God's given me. There is nothing wrong with that drive to be better and better as long as it is carried out in the right way with the right perspective."

—Tony Dungy

The Spirit of Excellence

Shaun Alexander
NFL Running Back

*Let your light shine before men, so that they may see your good works
and give glory to your Father in heaven.*

MATTHEW 5:16

Sports serve society by providing vivid examples of excellence.
GEORGE F. WILL

Excellence. That power-packed word can be found in catchphrases and taglines, heard in motivational speeches and printed on huge banners. It has been written about in countless books and has inspired major motion pictures. Athletes are especially fond of the word "excellence." The pursuit of it drives them to practice and train long hours. It compels them to discipline their bodies beyond the capacity of an average human being.

But what exactly is excellence? There seem to be many opinions on the topic but no one answer to that perplexing question. Within the world of sports, excellence tends to be measured by winning percentages, championship seasons and record-breaking performances. And while that is a somewhat skewed perspective, individuals and teams must give their absolute best efforts in order to accomplish great things.

NFL running back Shaun Alexander has learned that lesson playing for championship teams at every level—from high school to the pro ranks—and says that there was always an attitude of excellence and "a spirit where everybody was at the top of their game."

It's that spirit of excellence that Alexander has allowed to permeate his very existence. Therefore, excellence isn't just some unreachable lofty goal. It is instead a way of life. For Shaun Alexander, excellence is what he does. Alexander says achieving excellence requires obedience and purity of heart, which in turn inspire others to pursue excellence. But first, excellence requires what Alexander refers to as the attitude of perfection.

"Excellence is noble," he says. "It's first-rate. It's the highest form of honor. It's above normal. It's as high as you can get. I think of something that's worthy."

For Alexander, that attitude of perfection shows up on the football field as he gives that extra effort to reach the first-down marker, or at home when he rushes to the door to help his wife get the kids out of the car and bring the groceries to the kitchen. It's something he learned from influential people like his mother, Carol, and his legendary high-school football coach, Owen Hauck, who won 15 district titles and 12 regional championships at

25

Boone County High School in Florence, Kentucky. "Coach Hauck was committed to excellence," Alexander says. "He was like, 'People are going to know what we're going to do, and they won't be able to stop it because we're more committed to doing this thing precisely correct than they are to stopping it.'"

Hauck was a living, breathing example of commitment to excellence—the same kind of commitment Paul talked about in Ephesians 4:1 when he wrote, "I, therefore, the prisoner in the Lord, urge you to walk worthy of the calling you have received."

"That to me is saying we should walk in the spirit of excellence," Alexander says. This philosophy is contrary to an ever-growing belief found in today's world that, according to Alexander, states a Christian has to be weak. But according to 1 John 5:1-15—a passage that extols the benefits of being a believer—that twisted perspective is anything but true. In fact, in verse 5, John asks this rhetorical question: "Who is the one who conquers the world but the one who believes that Jesus is the Son of God?"

John emphasizes this thought later on in verses 14 and 15, where he shares this powerful promise: "Now this is the confidence we have before Him: whenever we ask anything according to His will, He hears us. And if we know that He hears whatever we ask, we know that we have what we have asked Him for."

To take it a step further, Alexander believes that excellence among Christians is not only a calling and a provisional blessing but also something that ultimately pleases God much the same way that excellence from a child pleases his or her parents. In both cases, a strong commitment to obedience is required, and that, Alexander says, is what really makes God happy.

"The best way to honor God is to be obedient," he says. "Whatever it is I'm doing, I want to be obedient. I want to pursue Him with excellence with all that I've got. That's going to lead into true obedience and true love, which pleases God.

"That's where our heavenly Father isn't like our earthly fathers. Our earthly fathers might get upset when we don't hit the game-winning shot, but our heavenly Father looks at our heart. If our heart is in the right place, He's going to be satisfied and say, 'Well done.' No matter how much your earthly father loves you, he still wants you to win the championship. But with God, the championship's already won."

While the ultimate purpose of excellence is to please God, there are other reasons for pursuing it. Excellence is one of the most effective tools for building God's kingdom because it involves having a disciplined work ethic and living a life of service to others. Jesus validated this concept in Matthew 5:14-16, one of the Gospel's most prominent passages: "You are the light of the world. A city situated on a hill cannot be hidden. No one lights a lamp and puts it under a basket, but rather on a lampstand, and it gives light for all who are in the house. In the same way, let your light shine before men, so that they may see your good works and give glory to your Father in heaven."

"When you listen to God, you can't help but do what He says, and you can't help but be that light and be that salt of the earth," Alexander says. "The spirit of excellence brings light because Jesus is light. When you're listening to Him and you're following Him and you're being obedient to Him, it just works."

Alexander has taken Jesus' words to heart as a mentor to many teenage boys. He can share numerous stories about how letting his light shine in both word and deed has made a significant spiritual impact.

"When I first got to Seattle, there were these junior-high kids who would always come to me to talk about Scriptures, and they'd ask me to give them Scriptures to memorize," Alexander says. "I knew they didn't know Jesus. But here they are now—they're seniors in high school—and eight of the kids are saved, on fire for Jesus, walking strong and being godly. How did that happen? I just developed a relationship with those kids.

"About two years ago—I've known them for six years now—they came to me and said, 'You know, Shaun, when we first met you, we weren't saved.' I was like, 'Really?' And they said, 'We just wanted you to sign autographs for us and our friends.' And I said, 'So you were just trading Scriptures for autographs?' And they said, 'Yeah, but we're all fired up now.' But I already knew that, and that's how it works. There are people who want to get close to you because they want something, and that's an opportunity to let your light shine."

For all of the significance that accompanies excellence, Alexander is also aware of the fact that this core value can also be perverted. This happens, for instance, when people who have been gifted with various talents and abilities use them for personal gain instead of for their intended purpose—to glorify God and draw people to Him. To illustrate this point, Alexander points to Paul's words found in Romans 11:29: "For the gifts and calling of God are without repentance" (*KJV*).

"You can be a gifted speaker," Alexander explains. "You can be a gifted football player. You can be taught the truth in the Bible and not follow it, but you've still got your gift. So what happens is you turn your gift into an idol. That's the greatest form of deception. You love the gift and not the giver."

The temptation to focus on the gifts that allow us to strive for excellence as opposed to giving all of our attention to God—the One who supplies those gifts—is something that we need to fight even at an early age. That's why Alexander has always made sure that his three daughters—Heaven, Trinity and Eden—know the difference between the two ways of thinking.

"When my daughter Heaven turned three, I bought her the first toy bike that she ever had. When she saw it, she ran right past the bike and jumped into my arms. That's because she loved the giver more than she loved

29

the gift. And I thought, *God, help me continue to teach her to love You more than the gifts that You've given her.*

Another temptation associated with excellence is to become so caught up in the pursuit of it and work so hard to attain it—even in the name of Jesus—that time isn't taken to get to know Him. Alexander says that's the same thing as giving it your all while working for a large organization but never taking time to learn more about your employer.

"Paul Allen was my boss when I played for the Seahawks," he says. "He's one of the richest men in the United States. If he walked into the locker room and saw me standing next to one of the guys on the practice squad, Mr. Allen would say, 'Hey, Shaun, how are you doing?' And I'd say, 'I'm good.' And he'd ask, 'Shaun, who's your friend here?' The friend would say, 'I'm on the team. I work for you.' And he would say, 'Oh, I'm sorry. Well, good luck this year.'

"The two of us guys were both wearing Seahawks' uniforms. We were getting paid from the same place. We both had the same goal—winning the Super Bowl. But there was one difference: I knew the head of the organization. To the other player, he was just the owner he worked for. People do the same thing with Jesus every day. They work for Jesus, but they don't really know Him."

At that point, the desire for excellence becomes an issue of motivation. Is it all about God or is it all about you? "Your motives reflect your heart," Alexander says.

"That's who you really are. For a lot of people, their motives are not godly. Their motives are selfish. At the end of the day, God's going to reveal the truth."

Having reached the pinnacle of success in the world of professional athletics, Alexander has been forced to check his motives on a regular basis. In particular, the 2005 NFL season provided numerous opportunities for him to ask some hard-hitting, introspective questions. In particular, he wanted to make sure he was giving God the glory—both publicly and privately—for his accomplishments, which included an NFL-leading 1,880 rushing yards, an NFL-record 28 total touchdowns (since broken by LaDainian Tomlinson), an appearance in Super Bowl XL (where the Seahawks lost to Pittsburgh) and the coveted NFL Most Valuable Player award.

"It's a dangerous thing anytime people start calling you valuable and it's not wrapped around Jesus Christ," Alexander says. "It's very easy to fall in that trap of thinking, *Now I'm something;* or, *Now I'm somebody.* It's honorable. I wouldn't mind being called MVP again next year. But at the same time, it really humbles me to say, 'Okay, God, I want to make sure that I'm Your MVP first.' A lot runs through your mind. You're shooting commercials. You're on top of billboards. Your book's coming out. All of the sudden you start believing that you're the world's MVP. But that's not the real goal. As exciting as it is, it also brings this soberness that when you're put up this high, it's even easier to fall off."

The Word of God bears out Alexander's sentiment. According to Proverbs 16:18, an oft-quoted Scripture, "pride comes before destruction, and an arrogant spirit before a fall."

Of course, sometimes it's just life that causes a fall. Such was the case for Alexander during the two seasons that followed his MVP performance. In 2006, he fractured the fourth metatarsal in his left foot during the third week and missed nearly three months of action. The 2007 season was just as devastating, as Alexander was plagued with a plethora of injuries, including a fractured left wrist, a twisted knee and a twisted ankle.

Throughout these difficult circumstances, however, Alexander continued to strive to give his best. While that wasn't always good enough for the fans or the media—who criticized him for a lack of effort (not realizing the severe pain he was playing with)—he says the true test of excellence is continuing to push toward the prize no matter what obstacles may be waiting ahead. Alexander is quick to point out that this requires honesty with yourself and others. "You have to learn to be real with yourself and be real with your brothers," he says. "Let's get back to the truth. The truth sets everybody free."

Alexander's paraphrase of John 8:32 ("You will know the truth, and the truth will set you free") points toward honesty—one of the more infrequently taught aspects of excellence. This in turn goes back to the issue of motivation. With that in mind, Alexander quotes Proverbs 28:13:

"The one who conceals his sins will not prosper, but whoever confesses and renounces them will find mercy."

"God's going to judge our hearts, and if you conceal sin, you're not going to prosper," Alexander says. "So be vulnerable. Learn how to be vulnerable with God. Learn how to be vulnerable with your buddies and your brothers and the ones who you're mentoring. I will get around people, and it doesn't take long for them to figure out that I'm much more about Jesus than I am about football or anything else."

Alexander is driven to be excellent as a football player, as a husband, as a father, as a philanthropist, as a mentor and, most importantly, as a worshiper and follower of God. That's because he understands the father-child relationship that His Creator wants to have with him. He wants to embrace God the Father with a passion, gratitude and thankfulness that recognizes the Giver of his gifts more than the gifts themselves. That's the kind of excellence that truly pleases God and can, in turn, make the biggest impact on others.

"The last thing He's going to say to us is, 'Well done, good and faithful servant,'" Alexander says. "That is a phrase of affirmation. You can't help but look at God as the Abba Father, because He's the One who's affirming us even to the end."

And until he hears those words for himself, Alexander will strive to walk out his life with the same spirit of excellence that he has carried thus far.

TRAINING TIME

1. Shaun Alexander talks about the excellence displayed by his high-school coach, Owen Hauck. Who are some hometown heroes who have inspired you because of their excellence? What qualities do they have that make them stand out in the crowd?

2. Read Ephesians 4:1-3. What callings are there on your life? What does the phrase "walk worthy of the calling you have received" mean to you? What are some concrete examples of how a person could follow Alexander's directive to "walk in the spirit of excellence"?

3. Read 1 John 5:1-15. What are some misconceptions people often have about Christians? What parts of this passage give you the courage to wholeheartedly pursue excellence? What are some things for which you should confidently ask God?

4. Read Romans 11:29. What happens to our talents and gifts if we misuse them? What are some ways we can use our gifts for selfish purposes? What are some ways that we can use those same gifts to glorify God?

5. Read Matthew 5:14-16. What are some ways that God has used excellence in your life as a light to attract others to Him? What are some other areas in your life where excellence could have a similar effect?

"When you strive for excellence, you are fulfilled in who you are, and you can have the greatest impact on the lives of others. I think the spirit of excellence helps us continue with everything we have so that we can get to the next test and pass it. Some people strive for excellence to glorify themselves or to look good in front of others. But if you have a spirit of excellence and you're doing what God has told you to do, you can't help but do something greater than you thought you could do and impact more people than you otherwise could have. Having a platform is one of my callings. There are some people whose spirit of excellence is to make sure that I'm elevated. I've got friends who no one ever hears about, and all they do is pray. But they pray with a spirit of excellence. That is their calling. So their spirit of excellence launches me to go walk in my spirit of excellence. It all works together. You have to know who you are in Christ. You have to know what God has called you to do. Then you have to do that with everything in you. The spirit of excellence causes you to affect people when you don't even know that they're watching. It's not about putting on your Sunday best, but it's about walking in that spirit of excellence. When people see that, they think, *This Jesus must be the real deal*."

—Shaun Alexander

3

THE PASSIONATE PURSUIT

Les Steckel
President and CEO of Fellowship of Christian Athletes

Brothers, I do not consider myself to have taken hold of it. But one thing I do: forgetting what is behind and reaching forward to what is ahead, I pursue as my goal the prize promised by God's heavenly call in Christ Jesus.

PHILIPPIANS 3:13-14

Desire is the key to motivation, but it's determination and commitment to an unrelenting pursuit of your goal—a commitment to excellence—that will enable you to attain the success you seek.

MARIO ANDRETTI

Throughout Les Steckel's 20 years as an NFL coach, he made stops in San Francisco, Minnesota, New England, Denver, Tennessee (via Houston), Tampa Bay and Buffalo. One place the president and CEO of Fellowship of Christian Athletes never coached was in Oakland, but something about that organization will always stick with him.

The Raiders (who spent 1982 through 1994 in Los Angeles) once bragged that they had more victories than any other professional football franchise. The team hung up huge banners all over its stadium touting that fact with catchphrases such as "Commitment to Excellence," "Pride and Poise" and "Just Win, Baby." But eventually, those signs became nothing more than faded reminders of a glorious but nonetheless diluted past.

"If you're going to be excellent, you always have to find ways to get better, and they never changed," Steckel explains. "They kept the same management. They kept the same assistant coaches, and they would always go hire a head coach who would come in and work with those assistant coaches who had been there 15 and 20 years. Everybody's in favor of progress. It's the changes they don't like. Excellence is something that people want, but it's hard to capture."

Before the pursuit of excellence can begin, however, a true understanding of its multilayered meaning must first take place—although Steckel's definition is pretty cut-and-dried. "Excellence is doing the very best with the gifts that God gave you," Steckel says. "Unfortunately, I don't think a lot of people wake up every day and say, 'How can I do my best today?' Why is the traffic always the fullest between 4 and 5:30? Because everybody left the office early, and they all want to get home. They're not saying, 'Hey, I can put a little more into my job. I want to do the best I can today.' But if you really want to have excellence in your life, you first have to look yourself in the mirror and ask yourself, *Am I really doing the best I can? Am*

I utilizing the talents that God gave me? I think that question is very simple. People know the answer. The problem is that they never ask themselves the question."

Perhaps one of the reasons people wrestle with excellence is because too often it is confused with perfection—something Steckel admits to often struggling with himself. "I don't want to go overboard, but I do want to please God," he says. "There's a difference between being perfect and pleasing Him."

And in order to truly please God, Steckel believes we must follow the exhortation found in 1 Peter 1:14-16: "As obedient children, do not be conformed to the desires of your former ignorance but, as the One who called you is holy, you also are to be holy in all your conduct; for it is written, Be holy, because I am holy."

"There was only one person who was perfect, and that was Jesus Christ," Steckel says. "But we still need to strive for excellence. Jesus is the best picture of excellence I can have. When Jesus came, He knew His mission, He was going to carry it out, and He didn't dance around it. He met it head on. He went to the cross. He knew what was going to happen, and He did it anyway. What a great example of excellence."

Not only do we have Christ's example of excellence, but we can also benefit from His comforting and heartening Spirit. In 2 Thessalonians 2:16-17, the apostle Paul gives credence to this truth: "May our Lord Jesus Christ himself and God our Father, who loved us and by his grace gave us eternal encouragement and good hope, encourage your hearts and strengthen you in every deed and word" (*NIV*).

"It's like the little kid who comes to his father and says, 'Daddy, I don't think I can do this,'" Steckel expounds. "So how does he respond? Does he say, 'Yeah, you're right. You can't do it.' Or does he say, 'Sure you can. Let me show you how you can do this.' A good dad will do that with his children. The heavenly Father can do that with His followers, but instead we try to do it ourselves. But you'll never acquire excellence when you try to do it apart from Christ."

According to Steckel, the pursuit of excellence must be intentional. It never just happens. There must always be a sense of purpose behind every decision that brings you closer to the goal. This is especially true in the sports world. "You can compete with yourself and strive to accomplish a goal or get better at what you're doing," Steckel says. "All athletes want to get better."

There's a great biblical example of intentionality found in the book of Daniel. At that time in Jewish history, Babylon had taken over Jerusalem and brought back to Babylon a group of "young men without any physical defect, good-looking, suitable for instruction in all wisdom, knowledgeable, perceptive, and capable of serving in the king's palace." Among the captives was Daniel along with Hananiah, Mishael and Azariah, who were respectively renamed Shadrach, Meshach and Abednego. Daniel was also given a new name: Belteshazzar. Although he accepted this new name, he decided from the beginning that he would not cave in to the traditions of Babylon but instead stay true to God.

Daniel 1:8 tells us that Daniel "determined that he would not defile himself with the king's food or with the wine he drank." Instead, he asked the chief official for permission for him and his friends to only eat vegetables and drink water for a 10-day period. At the end of the period, Daniel and his friends were in great health, so the official let them eat as they desired.

Then, in Daniel 1:17 we learn that "God gave these four young men knowledge and understanding in every kind of literature and wisdom. Daniel also understood visions and dreams of every kind." In other words, because they honored God with intentionality and determination, He in turn blessed them with excellence.

This mindset, of course, is the opposite of cutting corners—a practice that happens all too often in today's society. Steckel says people are usually bent toward taking the easy road, which makes the pursuit of excellence somewhat counter to human nature. As a coach, he has seen this manifested in even the simplest of tasks—such as athletes who run just inside the cones or boundary lines, even though such maneuvers only save them a step or two.

But God's Word tells us clearly what happens when corners are cut: "There is a way that seems right to a man, but its end is the way to death" (Proverbs 14:12). And the apostle Paul admonishes, "For whatever a man sows he will also reap" (Galatians 6:7). Self-deception and the abrogation of personal responsibility and discipline are at the opposite end of the spectrum from two attributes of excellence that Steckel believes are invaluable.

"The two most important qualities to have in achieving excellence are discipline and integrity," he says. "But more importantly, it's self-discipline and self-integrity. If you don't have those two qualities, I don't know if you'll ever see excellence. We know when we're doing right or wrong. It's just a matter of striving to be excellent."

Steckel's ideas about excellence didn't fully materialize until 1990, when he went through what he commonly refers to as his brokenness. Before that, he certainly strove for excellence but didn't have his pursuit in the proper biblical context.

"That's when I knew I was being called to excellence," Steckel recalls. "I'd never had the perspective of living for the Lord. I had these plans and I knew how I was going to go about it, and I knew God was right there with me, because He knew I had a good heart; and I never wanted to hurt anybody. I thought that's where I was headed."

While unemployed for the first time in his adult life, Steckel took the time to grow in his relationship with Christ. He listened to an audio series by Dr. Charles Stanley on the topic of brokenness and began to understand the truth found in Psalm 51:17: "The sacrifice pleasing to God is a broken spirit. God, You will not despise a broken

41

and humbled heart." He returned to the coaching ranks in 1991 at the University of Colorado (the same place he started his career in 1973) with a brand-new perspective and a properly focused pursuit of excellence.

"I still remember the pain and the heartache that I went through," Steckel says. "If you don't have that long, painful experience, you might not remember what you've learned. But if you wake up in the morning and can see the scars from the car wreck that God saved you from, that might work."

Since that time, Steckel has learned about the call to excellence that Paul wrote so eloquently about in Philippians 3:13-14: "Brothers, I do not consider myself to have taken hold of it. But one thing I do: forgetting what is behind and reaching forward to what is ahead, I pursue as my goal the prize promised by God's heavenly call in Christ Jesus."

And while many get caught up in the end result of excellence—which often is wrapped up in achievements and awards—Steckel believes that the journey is just as enriching and equally important.

"Reaching the goal may not be paramount, but striving to reach it is the greatest part," Steckel says. "The pursuit of excellence is so distorted in our society. I've coached with two teams that played in Super Bowls. Most people have never been to one. Both teams lost, and for months after we were treated like losers. How sad that is. We almost made it, but the response of the fellow players, the coaches and the media is that you're a loser. It's the same thing with the NCAA Final Four. You start with 65 teams and at the end 64 are losers and one is the winner. That's distorted.

"But there's nothing greater than the pursuit of excellence," he adds. "You may not reach it as an athletic team or as an individual athlete, but striving to get there is pretty rewarding."

As we begin to pursue excellence, something unique begins to take place. Others around us are inspired by our effort and our drive. Age doesn't factor into this process. Young and old alike can set positive examples of excellence for those around them.

"In order for people to experience that feeling of excellence, they need to have a model of excellence in their life," Steckel says. "That's where I believe that we as Christian men and women need to understand that each day we're a ministry that's on foot, and we have an opportunity to mentor athletes for a lifetime."

Paul stresses this concept in Philippians 3:16-17: "In any case, we should live up to whatever [truth] we have attained. Join in imitating me, brothers, and observe those who live according to the example you have in us."

"I was so blessed to work with athletes who went to the Pro Bowl and were First Team All-Americans," Steckel says. "They had the natural ability but didn't want to put in the extra effort. So my job was to push them to be the best. My number one hot button is helping someone else get better.

If I can help someone get better, I get really excited."

Steckel has often used three distinct methods for pushing others to excellence: attention, affirmation and affection. All of these must be distributed with impeccable consistency and discipline in order to be effective. Steckel saw the validity of this style of mentoring even in his earliest days when he was a young assistant coach with the San Francisco 49ers.

"I was 30 years old," Steckel says. "I had just begun coaching in the NFL. I was working on the field, learning drills and how to help players get better. I coached O. J. Simpson that year and a seasoned veteran like Gene Washington, who is now the executive director of the NFL. I used to tell Gene to come work on drills every Monday through Friday; and he'd say, 'Coach, we don't ever do anything in the off-season.' And I'd say, 'Well, you are. If you want to finish your career here, you'd better show up.' Boy, he hated me then, and now we're lifelong buddies. But I was showing him drills and doing things to help make him better."

And as you push others to get better, you must continually push yourself toward excellence as well. This comes through a prayerful relationship with God in which listening to His voice always trumps making your own voice heard. As you see excellence come to fruition in your life, Steckel believes it will draw you even closer to God and increase your passion for Him and the pursuit of His will for your life.

"When you get older, you appreciate what God has done for you," Steckel says. "You want to serve Him. As you go through life and you see how God has blessed you, you want to say, 'Hey, I'm ready to do it.' It's like the coach who says to the player, 'I'm going to take care of that for you. I'm going to get you that tutor so that you can do better in math. Don't worry. I'm going to get it done for you.'

"I can hear myself saying that to players all the time. So you get them what they need and now when they hit the field, what do you think they're going to do? Loaf? No, they'll bust their tail for you."

According to Steckel, the opposite of excellence is apathy. This is a dangerous state to be in for an athlete and even more so for a follower of Christ. The human body needs to be worked to get stronger, as opposed to a machine that gets weaker and weaker over years of hard use. As legendary Michigan Wolverines head coach Bo Schembechler used to say, "You're either getting better or you're getting worse."

Paul says it this way in Philippians 3:12: "Not that I have already reached [the goal] or am already fully mature, but I make every effort to take hold of it because I also have been taken hold of by Christ Jesus." Steckel echoes that sentiment and again is reminded of the Oakland Raiders, who once fell into the trap of believing they had obtained the highest level of excellence.

"You'll never arrive," he says. "There's no plateau."

TRAINING TIME

1. Les Steckel talks about the Oakland Raiders' struggle with change. In what ways do you struggle with change when it comes to training for competition or doing well at your job? What tools have you used to stay motivated in your pursuit of excellence?

2. Steckel says that most people tend to take shortcuts and give only what is required of them and no more. What are some examples of shortcuts people take in athletics, business, ministry and family life?

3. Read Daniel 1:1-21. How was Daniel intentional in his pursuit of excellence? What are some temptations to go with the crowd that we face today? What are some of the benefits of avoiding worldly living like Daniel and his three friends did?

4. Read Philippians 3:12-21. What are some things that can suppress our passionate pursuit of excellence? What encouragement does the apostle Paul give to help us overcome all such obstacles? What is the ultimate prize for those who strive for godly excellence?

5. How does Bo Schemnechler's comment, "You're either getting better or you're getting worse," agree or disagree with the mindset of most athletes today? How does knowing the pursuit of godly excellence never ends impact your ability to push through challenges?

"It's the little things. The little things add up. Do people spend time on what they do, or do they invest time? There's a tremendous difference. It's like the difference between a limited partnership and a general partnership. In a limited partnership, you might put $5,000 down, close your eyes and walk away. In a general partnership, you'll put $50,000 or $100,000 into it. You're going to be checking on that investment every week. So if you invest your life for Christ, it's going to be serious. The most important thing in your life is your close, intimate, personal relationship with Christ, period. That's it. God wants a relationship with people. He's a jealous God, and we're called to worship Him and bow to Him and call Him holy. When it comes to worship, I think too often it's all about a Sunday church service with great music, a nice sermon, a little bit of humor, shaking hands and having some coffee afterwards. But worship is about self-denial, suffering and sacrifice. If that's what we taught in the church, how many people would follow Christ? If you love the Lord, you should live for Him and please Him. If you know you're not pleasing Him in your actions, in your deeds, in your tasks, in your words, then do you really love Him? If you're trying to please Him, you'll strive for excellence. You'll strive to be the best that you can be. That's my motivation—to live for Him."

—Les Steckel

4

Good Habits

Albert Pujols
MLB First Baseman and Two-time NL MVP

Therefore, my dear brothers, be steadfast, immovable, always excelling in the Lord's work, knowing that your labor in the Lord is not in vain.

1 Corinthians 15:58

We are what we repeatedly do. Excellence, then, is not an act, but a habit.

Aristotle

Numbers. In sports, they often mean everything. Even the seemingly most inconsequential numbers can spell the difference between winning and losing—the difference between a gold medal and a silver medal, the difference between a championship and second place, the difference between greatness and mediocrity.

Numbers are especially important to professional athletes because things such as a league-leading scoring average or a consistent number of home runs can result in high-dollar contracts and job security.

But strangely, Albert Pujols (whose career numbers are eye-popping even to the average sports fan) could care less about his batting average, his RBI totals or his on-base percentage. "My goals every day are to help my team win and hopefully have the opportunity to go to the playoffs or the World Series," Pujols says. "That's my goal every year—to win the World Series. Through Christ, I get to please people through that because that's what we play for. God has blessed me to win a World Series in such a young career. After just seven years in the big leagues, playing in two World Series and six playoffs is just unbelievable. It's more than I could ask for. I really make sure I keep my eyes on Christ first. If I do that, I think everything else will be easy."

But for Pujols, growing up in a poor family in the Dominican Republic was anything but easy. He did what he could to help by taking odd jobs here and there, but Pujols mostly tried his best to work hard in school and stay out of trouble by playing baseball every afternoon in the streets. His family moved to the United States in the early 1990s and eventually settled in the Kansas City area. Pujols excelled in baseball at Fort Osage High School in Independence, Missouri, where he was a two-time All-State selection. He then played college ball at Maple Woods Community College where one season was enough to attract the attention of some Major League clubs.

Pujols was drafted by the St. Louis Cardinals in the thirteenth round of the 1999 draft, but he turned down a meager signing bonus and played that season in the Jayhawk League in Kansas. A year later, he was in the Cardinals' fold and headed to the minor leagues, where he spent

49

most of the 2000 season playing for the team's single-A club in Peoria. When Pujols started spring training in 2001, the Cardinals began to look for a way to include him on their 25-man roster. Once he took to the field that season, it became evident to all that Pujols would be a force to contend with for years to come.

But his Major League debut on April 2, 2001, is not even close to being the most important day in Pujols's life. That day had arrived three years earlier when he met his future wife, Deidre, a born-again Christian who invited him to church. Before that, Pujols had limited knowledge of the Bible and knew little more than the fact that "there was a guy who died for us."

He began attending a Bible study with Deidre at Kansas City Baptist Temple. As God softened his heart, Pujols's desire for a relationship with the Creator slowly grew until he could no longer resist. "There were times when I really wanted [to commit my life to Christ], but I never got a person to push me like my wife [did]," Pujols says. "It's like a lot of people believe it, but they don't want to get saved—they don't think they're ready. I think that day I was ready. I told my wife that when I walked into church that day, I was going to get saved."

Early on, Pujols called on Christian teammates such as Andy Benes, Mike Matheny and J. D. Drew for accountability and spiritual mentoring. Now, years later, Pujols is the one taking the role he once relied upon so heavily. "I'm growing in the Word right now, and God is showing me things," Pujols says. "If I hadn't accepted Christ when I first starting playing baseball, I don't know where I would be right now. It wasn't like I was a bad little boy. I never drank. I never smoked. I don't party. I don't do all of those things that people think you have to do to have fun in this life. There are other things that you can do to have fun in this world. People think that they need to go out and have a glass of wine or drink and all of that, but to me it's not important. I can have fun just going to the park and spending time with my family. I get to come home after a tough night at a stadium and see my kids laughing and spend time with them. That's more important to me."

Pujols's relationship with Christ has not only made him a better husband and father, but it has also helped strengthen him in his lifelong pursuit of excellence, a concept that he defines as "just doing the best that I can with what I do and then honoring God."

He was first inspired to strive for excellence when he was still in the Dominican Republic, initially by his large family and then later by the many professional baseball players who have emerged from his home country. Here in the United States, Pujols credits his wife, Diedre, for teaching him even more about excellence—specifically, excellence as it relates to the Word of God.

Rick Horton has had a front-row seat to Pujols's career since he burst onto the scene in 2001. Horton, a former St. Louis pitcher, is a member of the Cardinals' broadcast team and also serves as the area director for

Fellowship of Christian Athletes. He describes Pujols as "a miraculous athlete" with "incredible drive and determination." And he believes that Pujols's good habits—preparation, focus and discipline—separate him from the rest of the players.

"His preparation is beyond what most Major League Baseball players do," Horton says. "He really studies the film, and he's good at it. He studies the film of his opponents. He knows and understands the swing and breaks down the swing. He also hits more baseballs off the tee when nobody is looking than most players do. He really works at his craft. He's got a great work ethic. In all of the hoopla that's surrounded him over the years, he doesn't back down on his work. He just works harder. Every year going into spring training, he always says he's just trying to make the team; and everybody laughs when he says it because he's one of the best hitters on the planet, but at some deep level, he really means that."

Pujols literally takes nothing for granted. It doesn't matter to him that he won the 2001 National League (NL) Rookie of the Year award. It doesn't matter to him that he was named NL Most Valuable Player in both 2005 and 2008. It doesn't matter to him that he has the highest career batting average among active players. It doesn't matter to him that he's made multiple appearances in the All-Star Game (missing only the 2002 contest). It doesn't matter to him how many awards and big numbers he puts up. Pujols still approaches each season the same.

"Without preparation, you won't have excellence," Pujols says. "So I really try to prepare myself in the off-season for three months. I work hard in the gym and try to keep myself healthy. After you've laid the bat and glove down for three months, you can't just show up to spring training and expect to have excellence. It's impossible."

Horton believes that Pujols's consistent training is even more amazing considering the year-round demands on his time. "He's always at the park early," he says. "He's always doing something valuable. You never see him wasting time. He's also pretty focused. When he gets to the park, he goes about his business. Now he's got more business than everybody else does. A lot of players can't handle being the superstar. You're the team spokesman. Everybody wants to interview you. Players from the other team send you over a box of things to sign. It really does happen. I saw [Mark] McGwire go through that. It's unbelievable. But Pujols is impervious to distraction."

Pujols admits that it is very tough to stay focused. "There are a lot of distractions out there in this world right now," Pujols says. "There's women, drugs—everything. If you open the newspaper right now, you can see that every day there's something happening in this world. It's tough. I make sure that all of that doesn't get into my mind. I'm here to try to serve God and to try to honor Him and not get caught up in those distractions. Am I perfect? No. Nobody is perfect. Jesus Christ was the only One that was perfect. I just try to stay focused and make sure that whatever I do is to honor God. So those distractions are easy for me to avoid."

Preparation and focus, however, mean nothing without rock-solid discipline that is fortified by the will to succeed and to be excellent. Horton says that Pujols has stayed disciplined by establishing boundaries even when they can sometimes bring criticisms from those who don't understand (or respect) his need to stay true to specific training routines that provide mental, physical and spiritual balance.

"Albert's got pretty thick skin," Horton says. "He's totally immune to that. He knows who he is. He's comfortable with who he is. He's comfortable in his relationship with Christ, and he's doing what he can to grow personally and to lead others. He has had numerous occasions where he's presented his faith to his teammates and he knows he's accountable for that, but he's not trying to please men. I think that's helped him say no when he needed to say no and say yes when he needed to say yes."

As Pujols's spiritual life has grown exponentially, so has his understanding of the purpose for excellence on the baseball field, which also blends into his personal life, where his ability to impact others is just as significant.

"Now I live for Christ where before I was thinking about myself," Pujols says. "I've been saved since 1999, and I've seen how Christ has changed my life—how God has worked in my life and in my family. I see changed lives through [our Pujols Family Foundation] every day because God has given me the opportunity when before it was all about Albert Pujols. Now, through Christ, He has shown me that it's not about Albert Pujols. It's about Him. It's about helping others. I just thank God for allowing me to call on Him and for being my Father and for sending Jesus to die on the cross for my sins and for giving me the opportunity to leave that selfishness I had in the past and to live for Him right now."

Furthermore, Pujols contends that because of his daily commitment to excellence, he now has the opportunity to share the message of salvation through Christ with others—teammates, team administrators and fans—who otherwise would not be as receptive to him.

"You have to set an example of excellence," Pujols says. "If you were the average guy and you go out there and don't take care of your business and you don't do the things you're supposed to do and you don't lead by example—which is what God wants us to do—you're not going to have the opportunity to witness. If they see me doing crazy things, they're going to say, 'What are you talking about? You're just doing the same things that I'm doing.' But I have to set an example in the clubhouse. I'm not perfect. The only One who was perfect was Christ. We want to be perfect. We want to be like Him, but that's impossible because if we were perfect, we wouldn't be here right now."

Pujols has used his platform as a star player to influence his teammates and share the hope of eternal life with them. "I have a really good relationship with Yadier

[Molina]," he says. "I thank God that He gave me the opportunity about three years ago to witness to him, and he gave his life for Christ. To me, that's bigger than hitting a home run in game seven of the World Series with two outs in the bottom of the ninth. That was the best thing that happened to me that year—knowing that I witnessed to one of my teammates, a guy who I really admire and a guy who I really tried to help."

Pujols also displays his commitment to excellence off the field through the Pujols Family Foundation, which he runs with his wife. They work to support families touched by Down syndrome, in part due to the fact that his adopted daughter, Isabella (born to Deidre prior to their marriage in 2000), was born with the condition. Through the foundation, the Pujols family also actively supports many programs aimed at improving the education, economic situation and physical environment of impoverished children and their families in the Dominican Republic. He and his wife also make an annual medical missions trip to his native country during the off-season.

"Knowing the Word of God and going back to the Dominican Republic, I'm able to teach people about what God has done in my life, and I'm able to set an example and show them who I live for," Pujols says. "Christ is using me through the foundation, so I can witness to people who don't know the Word. They listen because I'm Albert Pujols the baseball player. Well, it's not about Albert

Pujols. It's about Christ. Every day I thank God for that. He could have picked anyone, but I'm grateful and thankful that He's using me to reach these poor kids in the Dominican Republic who don't have anything."

"[Pujols] talks a lot about his responsibility to do his best with the gifts God has given him," Horton adds. "He says that publicly all the time. I think he's got a really good understanding of stewardship. We always think about that as a financial thing, but it's primarily a giftedness issue. He uses his gifts and his finances. I think that's part of his spiritual growth that keeps him connected. He's also growing in his leadership. It's pretty evident in the Cardinal clubhouse."

That's just another reason why Pujols believes excellence has little to do with numbers and everything to do with giving all you have to the glory of God. His philosophy can be traced back to Hebrews 13:15-16, which says, "Therefore, through Him let us continually offer up to God a sacrifice of praise, that is, the fruit of our lips that confess His name. Don't neglect to do good and to share, for God is pleased with such sacrifices."

"I haven't done anything to deserve what God has given me," Pujols says. "I really enjoy my relationship with Him and I enjoy my family and I enjoy this game. I'm having fun with this game. This is a platform that He has given me, so I can glorify Him and I can witness to other people. I make sure that I do my 110 percent and do my best to honor Him."

TRAINING TIME

1. Numbers have an important place in athletics and other areas of life. What are some ways that numbers impact the difference between success and failure in your life? How closely do you keep up with your numbers? Does the way you approach statistical information help or hinder your performance?

2. For Pujols, the pursuit of excellence starts with preparation. What are some ways that you prepare for competition? Read Ephesians 6:10-18. How is a soldier's preparation similar to that of a competitor? What are some consequences of being unprepared?

3. Read 1 Corinthians 15:58. What are some distractions you deal with on a daily basis? How does Paul encourage us to avoid such distractions? What do you think "your labor in the Lord is not in vain" means?

4. Read Proverbs 21:31. What motivates you to have good habits as an athlete? In other areas of your life? How disappointed are you when you don't win or don't achieve your goals? How does the passage in Proverbs keep performance results in perspective?

5. Read Hebrews 13:15-16. In what ways are good habits "a sacrifice of praise" (v. 15)? How does placing God at the top of your priority list keep you focused on striving for excellence?

"One of my good friends is Mark Cahill. He wrote a book called *One Thing You Can't Do in Heaven*. Back during the 2006 season, he challenged me. He said, 'Albert, I know it's a tough year, but God has promised you more. For every guy who gets on first base, ask them questions about who Jesus is: What do you think is going to happen to you when you die? If you died today, where do you think you're going to go? And just ask them questions and have fun.' As I was struggling, that's what I did. It was after the All-Star break, and I started doing that. I started witnessing to people at first base, even though they might be there for only a few seconds. You'd be surprised how many people I witnessed to at first base. Some of them were Christians, and I encouraged them to do the same thing at their position or in the dugout with their teammates. There were some who would say their family was the most important thing in their life or money or baseball, and I'd say, 'You're wrong.' Then I would grab one of Mark's books and send it to them, and if I had the time before batting practice, I'd try to spend some time with them and try to witness to them."

—Albert Pujols

5

PUSHING THROUGH

Jean Driscoll
Former Olympic and Paralympic Wheelchair Athlete

Rejoice in hope; be patient in affliction; be persistent in prayer.

ROMANS 12:12

Persistence is the twin sister of excellence. One is a matter of quality; the other, a matter of time.

MARABEL MORGAN

When Jean Driscoll was a teenager, she had all of the same negative ideas about wheelchairs as everyone else. They were cumbersome and limiting, and using one meant the end of any shot at a normal life. And that's exactly how she felt when, as a high school sophomore, she was forced to use one herself.

"I thought my life was over," Driscoll candidly says.

It took another 10 to 15 years for Driscoll, whose condition was caused by spina bifida, to learn that her life was in fact *not* over. It was just beginning. And then in 2002 at a Bible study, she stumbled across Daniel 7:9—a passage that confirmed what God had been revealing to her all along: "As I kept watching, thrones were set in place, and the Ancient of Days took His seat. His clothing was white like snow, and the hair of His head like whitest wool. His throne was flaming fire; its wheels were blazing fire."

By then, Driscoll had already come to understand the purpose behind her disability. Many years of life experience and spiritual growth separated her from the pain, hurt and confusion that surrounded her childhood and teenage years. But that didn't make her discovery any less inspiring.

"Daniel is giving a description of God," Driscoll explains. "It says that there are wheels on His throne, and then it says there's fire coming out from behind it. Not only does God's throne have wheels, He burns rubber! Anytime I've had an opportunity to talk with people who use wheelchairs and feel bad about being in a chair, I tell them, 'Not only are you made in the image of God, but your wheelchair is made in the image of His throne!'"

When Driscoll was growing up in Milwaukee, Wisconsin, there was no one around to give her that same kind of encouragement. At the time of her birth in 1966, nearly half of the babies born with spina bifida (a birth defect that results in improper development of the spine) died due to infection or some other complication. Even though her case was relatively mild, she still needed to wear leg braces, and she struggled with balance.

"My feet turned out to the side, and I would sway back and forth," Driscoll says. "Because I walked so awkwardly, I got stared at a lot. I got teased a lot. So I grew up

61

not having good self-esteem and not feeling good about myself. I always felt frustrated because my body didn't work like everybody else's. I would try to be involved in different sports activities, but my legs were not strong enough. So I was the scorekeeper for our grade-school volleyball team, and I was the manager of the girl's basketball team, but I never really got to get in there and get dirty."

Driscoll dealt with her challenges as best as she could under the circumstances. But as a child of the 1970s, there was still a long way to go in terms of technological advancements and public support for people with disabilities. Unfortunately, Driscoll's life became even more difficult during her freshman year at high school when she crashed her newly acquired bicycle on the way home from a babysitting job. Driscoll took a hard fall, and because of her weak lower-body muscles, she dislocated her hip. That tragic mishap led to five major operations over the next year and required her to wear a body cast that covered three-fourths of her body.

"It was a really long year. . . . I spent a lot of time by myself," Driscoll says. "I remember praying over and over and over again that maybe after all of these surgeries were over, my feet would point forward instead of out to the side and it would be one more way that I would be like everybody else. I just wanted to be like everybody else. That was my goal. I wanted to blend in. I hated sticking out."

She was sent home to recover and work on flexibility, but over the course of two weeks, her hip again became dislocated. None of the surgeries had worked and now came the inevitable: first crutches and eventually the dreaded wheelchair.

"I was so mad at God because I thought that He was picking on me," Driscoll says. "First, I was born with this disability and I was constantly teased, and then I had all of these painful surgeries. I've got foot-long scars over both hips. None of those surgeries worked, and doctors are supposed to be able to fix everything. I didn't understand why they couldn't fix my body. It was really a hard time."

But Driscoll had no idea that God would use the wheelchair and her disability to open doors to some incredible and unimaginable places. Her journey began as a high-school junior when she met a young man who also had spina bifida and used a wheelchair. He invited Driscoll to play wheelchair soccer, which was one of many adapted sports that were becoming increasingly popular with people who used wheelchairs.

With an array of stereotypes dominating her mind, Driscoll wanted no part of what she assumed was an inferior knockoff of the real deal. She eventually did, however, go to observe a practice, where she was surprised at the intense and fierce competition she saw. Driscoll's instant intrigue led her to discover a wide range of wheelchair sports, including ice hockey, football, softball, tennis and basketball. It was the last, wheelchair basketball, that brought her to the University of Illinois—a move that she says changed her life.

Driscoll was at home one day when she saw the women's 800-meter wheelchair race at the 1984 Summer Olympics in Los Angeles being broadcast live on television. Her family didn't watch sports much, but somehow she was walking by the television, on her crutches, just as Sharon Hedrick won that historic race. Driscoll was captivated by it all but still had no idea that she would soon be heading down the same path. Then she was recruited to play wheelchair basketball by the University of Illinois, where her coach was Brad Hedrick, the husband of the woman Driscoll had watched make Olympic history by winning the first Olympic gold medal awarded to a wheelchair athlete.

At Illinois, Driscoll added track and road racing to her collegiate repertoire. That's where she began working with another key figure in her life—Marty Morse, coach of the University of Illinois wheelchair track and field. After a string of successful road races that ranged from 5K to 12K, Morse tried to talk Driscoll into competing in a marathon. Initially, she was fearful of the distance and had no desire to do so. But she finally gave in and raced at the Chicago Marathon. Driscoll's surprising second-place finish qualified her for the prestigious Boston Marathon, although she again wasn't terribly thrilled at the idea of racing such a long distance.

From there, however, her competitive life took flight. She not only won the 1990 Boston Marathon but also broke the world record. Driscoll went on to win seven consecutive Boston Marathons and an eighth race in 2000. She set new world marks a total of five times.

Driscoll also found great success at the Olympic Games, where she won silver in the 800-meter Women's Wheelchair Exhibition Event at the 1992 and 1996 Olympics in Barcelona and Atlanta. From 1988 to 2000, she competed in four consecutive Paralympic Games and won a total of five gold medals, three silver medals and four bronze medals.

In the early years of her transformation, Driscoll still struggled with identity and purpose. Her understanding of God was skewed by tragedy and tumult. "I always felt like I was being punished because God was a big, mad God and if you did things wrong, He was going to get you," Driscoll says. "My question was, Why is He only calling me out? Why isn't He ever mad at my siblings?"

As Driscoll's legend grew, so did her relationship with some people who God was placing in her life. An athletic administrator at Illinois named Debbie Richardson was one key individual who invited her to church and introduced her to Fellowship of Christian Athletes. It was a slow process for Driscoll, but by the time she had won her third Boston Marathon in 1992, she finally started to acknowledge God's part in all of it.

"I started to see a God who wasn't constantly judgmental, constantly angry, constantly punishing me," Driscoll says. "It broke those chains on my heart. It was such a freeing experience."

When Driscoll surrendered her heart and her life to Christ, the passionate pursuit of excellence came into clearer focus. She had always defined excellence as "giving your all" but now understood for whom her excellence was truly intended.

"In 1992, I started looking back, and it was a very short racing career to that point; but the success that I had experienced was phenomenal," Driscoll says. "I started looking at things that God had placed in my life. I started to see my disability more in terms of a workout and training. When I was younger and able to walk, it took all the energy I had. I would be exhausted after even short distances, but it helped me develop other areas in my life like mental toughness and never quitting, because I was always trying to keep up with everybody else."

Later on in her spiritual journey, Driscoll was writing down her thoughts for a speech at a Christian organization and came to an even deeper realization of God's plan for her life. "All of those early years when I was being picked on and I thought that God was picking on me, I was so tired of being picked on," Driscoll says. "Then I realized that I had been picked *out*. I had been picked out to do things that God only created me to do. I was working so hard to blend in and be like everybody else, and He kept pulling me out and showing me that I wasn't like everybody else. My life was not meant to blend in, but it was meant to stand out. That just blew me away—and it still does."

As Driscoll grew in her faith, she began to understand the correlation between the Bible and her growing physical and mental strength. Romans 12:12 has been a particularly inspirational Scripture in her quest for excellence: "Rejoice in hope; be patient in affliction; be persistent in prayer."

"Perseverance has been one of those things at my core," Driscoll says. "It took me two or three times the effort to do what everyone else was doing. That has stuck with me throughout my life. It's one of those things that God was cultivating in me without my even realizing it. So as I have moved through different experiences of life and different seasons of life, certainly athletics was huge and still is such a part of my success story, but perseverance had everything to do with my ability to get through those workouts, whether I was feeling strong or whether I was feeling weak."

Personal experience has revealed another truth to Driscoll: excellence requires some level of perseverance, and perseverance is ultimately fueled by hope.

"I don't think you can have excellence without perseverance," she says. "I think the two things work together. There are other qualities that are folded in that too. Hope has a lot to do with perseverance. The Bible tells us that the greatest gifts are faith, hope and love, with love being the greatest—but hope is huge. Hope is what makes or breaks people. You can't persevere without having that hope of what's to come."

But perseverance isn't just a matter of stiffening one's neck and bulldozing through adversity. Driscoll says there are a number of hindrances to perseverance that make it all too easy for people to give up on themselves.

"I believe our biggest limitations are the ones that we place on ourselves or the ones that we allow others to place on us," Driscoll says. "So often people are told you can't do this and you can't do that. Growing up with a disability, you constantly hear people putting you down. When people place limitations and negative talk on people, it can be a huge hindrance. But also our own negative talk and our own self-imposed limitations keep us from doing things."

It's hard to say which is the greater tragedy: people who raise the white flag and fail to see their dreams through or people who persevere but then take the credit and refuse to acknowledge God throughout the process. Driscoll believes that the latter is usually motivated by the insecurity that results from emptiness, sadness and loneliness. On the flip side, it's those who readily seek help and cry out in their time of need who often find a portal to divine strength and grace.

"There's a freedom in being able to reach out to others in your own weakness," Driscoll says. "That's exactly what God calls us to do. He wants us to bring our weakness. He wants us to come to Him, and He will give us strength. He is the gift of life. So you don't have to rely on yourself. It doesn't take as much energy to get through life, and you have a brighter perspective."

Driscoll has learned all of these things as part of her own lifelong journey from physical brokenness to spiritual wholeness. She readily shares the message of hope with all who will listen, but her story has proven especially powerful to disabled individuals in such developing countries as Ghana, where Raphael Nkegbe and Ajara Busanga are among those whose lives Driscoll has touched.

"That's the gift that I'm able to give to those people with disabilities in Africa right now," she says. "In many parts of Africa, individuals with disabilities are seen as being cursed by God. They have no value. They're considered to be like the dogs that run around on the ground. It's so opposite of what the Bible says."

Driscoll made her first trip to Ghana in 2001. She introduced wheelchair racing to Nkegbe and Busanga, who have since developed into world-class athletes. Both of them competed at the 2004 Paralympics in Athens, and Busanga won a gold medal at the 2008 All Africa Games. More importantly, both of them went from being outcasts to receiving celebrity treatment in their home country.

And none of this would have been possible had Driscoll not persevered and continued to strive for excellence in every facet of her life.

"God has given me a platform that reaches other continents," Driscoll says. "I couldn't even walk a block to my own school. It's tremendously humbling to think that God trusts me with all of this. What an incredible honor—and what joy."

TRAINING TIME

1. What are some personal challenges or physical limitations that you have dealt with? Did you ever feel like giving up? What was it that gave you the strength to fight through those times?

2. Jean Driscoll had several people in her life who pushed her to achieve great things—even when she didn't believe in herself. Who are some people who have been encouragers throughout your career and your life in general? In what ways did they give you support and inspiration? When have you been able to fill that role for someone else?

3. Driscoll says that her disability helped her to develop mental toughness. What does mental toughness mean to you? Do you consider yourself mentally tough? If so, what has helped you develop that quality?

4. Read Romans 12:12. What do you think it means to "be patient in affliction"? In what ways do your trials push you to excellence? What are some trying circumstances you've faced in your life that forced you to be patient? How did dealing with those situations impact your ability to handle any challenges that followed?

5. Read John 17:4. In what ways did Jesus persevere in order to bring glory to God? What are some ways that you can glorify God through perseverance?

"Just to get my coach Marty Morse off my back, I told him I'd do one marathon. We started training for the Chicago Marathon, which was in October of 1989. I couldn't wait until it was over, because I hated the training. The mileage was twice as long and the workouts were twice as long. The night before the race I couldn't sleep. I was so fearful of the distance. My goal was to stay with my teammate, Ann Cody, as long as I could. In our workouts, she would get away from me after the first couple of miles, and I would have to finish the workout alone. I was able to stay with her the first 20 miles, and I finished in second place, eight seconds under two hours. Then Marty told me I'd qualified for the Boston Marathon. My heart sank, because I didn't want to do another marathon. But the following spring I was in Boston. The race started, and I was among the top three women who had broken away from the pack. Then I got away from the girl who had won the Boston Marathon and broken the world record the year before. When I came across the finish line, not only did I win, but I broke the world record by almost seven minutes. And I didn't think I belonged in the race. It was a breakthrough experience. Marty saw something in me that I hadn't seen in myself."

—Jean Driscoll

6

RAISING THE STANDARD

Chris Klein
MLS Midfielder

*Finally then, brethren, we request and exhort you in the Lord Jesus,
that as you received from us instruction as to how you ought to walk
and please God (just as you actually do walk), that you excel still more.*

1 THESSALONIANS 4:1, *NASB*

*Success will not lower its standard to us. We must raise our
standard to success.*

RANDALL R. MCBRIDE, JR.

One athlete's career-threatening injury is another athlete's blessing in disguise. At least that's been the case for Major League Soccer veteran and four-time All-Star Chris Klein, who tore his right anterior cruciate ligament (ACL) in 2001 and his left ACL in 2004.

Both times, Klein made spectacular returns to the field and deservedly earned Comeback Player of the Year honors (2002 and 2005). Although each injury was potentially career ending, he leaned heavily on his relationship with God and a strong desire to show the league and its fans the true meaning of excellence. "Right after that first knee injury, I had a peace in knowing that God had a plan for me," Klein says. "That allowed me to put the work into my rehab and come back from the injury and be a better soccer player. With those two injuries, I've had more of an opportunity to speak about my faith than anything else I've done on the field in my entire career. I look back on those injuries and wouldn't trade them."

A few years earlier, Klein might not have displayed the same positive outlook. Although he grew up in a home where the Bible was taught, he says that in high school, college and the early part of his professional career, sports "became all-consuming and it was all about the performance on the field. It was about scoring the goal or winning or getting my name in the paper and doing all of those things."

At Indiana University, Klein led the Hoosiers to the NCAA semifinals, where his team lost to UCLA, the eventual champions, 1-0. It was Indiana's only loss of the season (23-1). As his college career came to an end, a new life with his wife, Angela, was about to begin. Her influence helped him understand the need for salvation through Jesus, and he began immersing himself in God's Word and engaging in the long, deliberate process of surrender.

At about the same time, Klein was selected by the Kansas City Wizards as the fourth overall pick in the 1998 MLS college draft. Despite playing at a high level for most of his athletic career, Klein was about to experience an even higher level of competitive pressure as a member of talent-rich Major League Soccer and eventually as an occasional member of the U.S. National Team. He spent eight seasons with the Wizards and was part of the 2000 MLS championship team. He then played one-and-a-half seasons for Salt Lake Real before being traded to the Los Angeles Galaxy in 2007, where he now shares the field with international megastar David Beckham and U.S. National Team legend Landon Donovan.

"There are a lot of stresses that go along with being a professional athlete," Klein says. "It's a very up-and-down job. You could have the best game of your life one week, and the very next week you could have the worst game of your life. It's that inconsistency—without faith in Jesus Christ—that would really put me way up and down. It helps to know that I'm not playing to do interviews or for the coach or for the fans. All of those things are great, but the real glory comes in playing for Christ."

As Klein grew in his spiritual walk, his ideas about excellence were challenged. One defining moment came when he heard a sermon that extolled the concept of living life for an audience of One. "That's true excellence to me—seeing that picture of just Jesus sitting in the stands," Klein says. "I know that He loves us always and loves us unconditionally, but I always ask the question, 'Is He smiling at me or is He shaking His head?' It's that sort of idea that helps me strive to be excellent every day, whether people are watching or whether no one is watching."

Even before he came to that understanding, the groundwork for excellence was laid by his father, Rich Klein, who taught his son to "play fair" and "play hard."

"I've also been very fortunate to have some great coaches in my career who really knew how to motivate on the field, but who really knew what character meant and how to build character through sports," Klein says. "It started with my high-school coach, Greg Vitello, in St. Louis and then on to college with Coach [Jerry] Yeagley at Indiana. These guys knew the game of soccer, but I learned more about how to be a man through those two men than anything I learned on the field. I believe that has a lot to do with the success I've had at the professional level."

Perhaps just as important in his spiritual growth was his ability to rub shoulders with Fellowship of Christian Athletes' national leadership in Kansas City during his time with the Wizards. Klein was introduced to the ministry by his mother-in-law, Carol Messerli, who has been involved with FCA in Eden Prairie, Minnesota, for several years. "FCA piqued my interest for sure—the way they pair sports and faith, especially with what I do for a living," Klein recalls. "To see that reflected in kids at such an impressionable time in their lives, it just sort of resonated with me."

FCA's influence helped solidify Klein's renewed perspective on excellence. He had long since figured out the physical and emotional sides of the concept but now had the spiritual element firmly in its rightful place.

"When it comes to excellence, I have to look at everything through God's eyes," Klein says. "I look at who Jesus was as the ultimate example of excellence and service and humility and all of those values. I look at Him, and I obviously fall short of each of those in comparison to Him. God has given me a talent and an ability to play soccer and to be excellent in doing that—to strive to be like Jesus when I'm out on the field, when I'm at home with my family, when I'm walking on the street, when I'm driving my car. So my ultimate definition of excellence is striving to be like Jesus."

At the same time, Klein is well aware of the truth found in Romans 3:23: "For all have sinned and fall short of the glory of God."

"But that doesn't mean we should stop striving for excellence," he says. "I think when we give up on that, we sort of miss the whole concept that Jesus teaches us. And I think especially in sports, there comes that misconception that as Christian athletes, maybe you get too nice or you don't want to compete. But for me, it's about that competition. It's about competing as hard as I can for His glory. It's not for my glory but for where He wants to take me in life. That's really what drives me to continue."

For Klein, there are numerous biblical references to excellence that back up that desire. Romans 12:1 is one of his personal favorites: "By the mercies of God, I urge you to present your bodies as a living sacrifice, holy and pleasing to God; this is your spiritual worship."

"I look at singers who praise Jesus when they sing, and that's just the ultimate act of worship for me," Klein says. "I don't sing very well, but I do play soccer. So I have that idea of offering this sacrifice to Him each game I play. He gave me this talent, and for me to offer it back up to Him is my way of worshiping. I certainly love listening to music but being able to express myself and to glorify Him on the field can become my sacrifice."

Another one of Klein's inspirational Scriptures is Colossians 3:23-24: "Whatever you do, do it enthusiastically, as something done for the Lord and not for men, knowing that you will receive the reward of an inheritance from the Lord—you serve the Lord Christ."

"It's that idea of striving toward excellence for Jesus and not for men," he says. "If I'm able to strive for excellence in Jesus' eyes, it's going to affect men also. But my first priority has to be to give my life over to Him, and that's going to spill over to other people."

In order to be excellent, Klein believes that a person first must determine to raise the standard in every aspect of life. In 1 Thessalonians 4:1, Paul tells the church members in Thessalonica "to walk and please God . . . that you excel still more" (*NASB*). And for the perfect example of how to "walk and please God," Klein suggests an obvious yet too-often overlooked model of excellence.

"When you talk about a standard of living, it comes back to Jesus for me," Klein says. "He is the standard. Each day, we can raise the bar, but we're never going to reach that standard. But it's the pursuit of that standard and continually raising the bar that we have to strive for every day. When we give up on that pursuit, we've given up on our faith. When anyone talks about raising the bar, it's going to that extra level to glorify Him. When your eyes are set on an eternal prize, I think that you continually raise the bar of excellence in your earthly life."

So what does raising the standard or raising the bar of excellence look like? While there's not likely to be a uniform answer that everyone can easily agree on, Klein has an idea of what might be the most important first step for himself.

"I need routine in my life," he says. "So for me, my spiritual day starts out with waking up and giving my life to Him right off the bat. Sometimes I find that if I don't sit down and have some quiet time by myself before I start my day, it's like I'm trying to do it on my own, and I notice the difference throughout the day. So I try to get up before anyone else in the house gets up and have time in prayer and have time studying and reading God's Word. That jump-starts me and gets my mind in the right framework so that I can go out and serve others and be more like Him."

Another step toward excellence takes Klein to—of all places—the kitchen. That's where he makes sure to properly feed his physical self. "As I get older playing this sport, taking care of my body becomes that much more important to me," Klein says. "Putting good things into my body is the fuel for what I go out and do. The most important thing for me in the morning is to energize my mind by reading God's Word and also to energize my body by putting the right things in there so that I can perform on the field."

As Klein ticks off his list of ways to raise the bar, however, he continues to focus on more personal matters. In fact, his next priority (like the previous two) is rooted within the home setting, where he says being an example to his wife and children (Carson and Cami) plays a vital role in the pursuit of excellence.

"You can see it in young kids," Klein explains. "What they see you do, they mimic. Sometimes it really gives you an eye-opening experience when you hear something come out of their mouths or you see something they do that you can see in yourself and that you don't want to see in your kids. That's why my wife and I make our marriage our priority, and hopefully that makes us better parents."

Klein believes that focusing on internal matters of excellence ultimately spills over into other areas of a person's life. For him, that translates into tangible opportunities to serve as a living, breathing witness of God's sovereignty and providence. But that can only happen if a person chooses to follow Christ's example of humility.

"For me, it might be going into the locker room and doing things that people may not expect, like bringing someone a newspaper or bringing someone a cup of coffee," Klein says. "At home, maybe it's rubbing my wife's back or giving my kids a hug or just keeping that idea of service at the forefront of my mind. It helps me to be the better husband, the better teammate and the better friend. Living my life that way is what drives me."

In his quest for excellence, Klein admits that there are numerous forces (both external and internal) that sometimes stand between him and his goals—forces that most everyone tends to face on a daily basis.

"It feels good when people are talking about you in a positive way," Klein says. "Sometimes you can kind of puff your chest out when you have a good game or when you see your name in the paper. Taking ownership of that is something that hinders me. Another thing is the busyness of life and not being able to just enjoy it and be appreciative of what God has given us. Worry can also be a big hindrance. Worrying about what the future holds can take you out of the mode of fully trusting in Him. For me, that becomes a big roadblock in my life."

As a highly disciplined professional athlete, Klein says the key to maneuvering past such hurdles ultimately leads back to his first priority: a daily commitment to Bible devotion, prayer and listening for God's voice. It's that rock-solid foundation that brings peace, understanding and trust, no matter what uncertainties life may bring.

"Being traded from one team to another and wondering what my life is going to look like in another city is a scary thing—especially when you have a wife and two kids who you're going to drag along with you," Klein says. "But having that trust of being part of God's plan and letting Him use me as a tool for His glory—thinking of my life in that context—really keeps me going and keeps my feet moving."

Another thing that energizes and motivates Klein to continually raise the standard is the opportunity he often has to share his faith with others—whether that is his teammates, others who work for the team, soccer fans, or kids who he speaks to in schools and in youth groups.

"Hopefully it becomes who you are," Klein says. "Athletes are role models. High-school athletes are role models. The seniors are role models to the juniors. The juniors are role models to the sophomores. Whether we like it or not, we're role models. So then it becomes a choice for me. Am I going to choose to be a positive role model or am I going to choose to be that guy who I don't want to be?"

And in order to be the role model God has called him to be, Klein believes that excellence along with the other FCA core values—serving, integrity and teamwork—are required in order to make the biggest impact on his family, his friends, his teammates and his fans.

"These core values are things that last," Klein says. "These are things that will go from one game to the next, from one season to the next, from one career to the next. If I have a good game, I have to start all over the next week because there's another one coming. These core values transcend what you do on the field."

TRAINING TIME

1. In your sport or field of interest, who are some fig-
   ures that have set the highest standards? What are
   some of the attributes that make those individuals
   special? In what ways does seeing them in action motivate you to strive to give your best?

2. Read Romans 12:1. Chris Klein says his soccer career is
   "about competing as hard as I can for His glory." How
   does his philosophy line up with the mentality of
   many athletes today? What do you find most challenging about the exhortation found in Romans 12:1?

3. Read Colossians 3:23-24. How does this passage re-
   inforce Klein's idea about playing for an audience of
   One? Is playing or working for God's approval as opposed to man's approval more stressful or less stressful? Why so?

4. Read 1 Thessalonians 4:1-12. What are some ways
   the apostle Paul encourages us to raise the standard?
   How can living by a high standard of morality and
   righteousness bring excellence into all areas of life?

5. Klein says that Jesus was "the ultimate example of excellence and service and humility." What are some
   other ways in which Jesus modeled excellence for us?
   How can striving to live like Him make us better athletes and ministers of the gospel?

"Sometimes humility might seem to stand at the opposite end of the spectrum from excellence. But for me, they sort of collide. Jesus' example is something that I strive for. I play a team sport. If you're only thinking about yourself, you will be detrimental to a team. But if your idea going into a practice or a game is, God, please help me to serve my teammates today, it's that idea of being there for them and supporting them during the game and trying to make the other players better. The best soccer players in the world are those who make others around them better. It's the idea of service and humility that I think makes the most excellent soccer player. It's all about wanting to serve your teammates in the locker room, wanting to get to know them, wanting to love them, wanting to hear about their lives. I think it makes for a better team atmosphere, and it makes me a better teammate. I hope that the way I live my life—especially in a team atmosphere—and the way they look at me makes them think, Maybe this is the better way to do it. When that sort of atmosphere gets injected into a team, you hope that it affects other guys and becomes the standard for a team. The best teams that I've been on have not had the best players or the biggest stars, but they've played the best together."

—Chris Klein

LASTING LEGACIES

Richard and Kyle Petty
NASCAR Stock-Car Drivers

---

*God, You have heard my vows; You have given a heritage to those
who fear Your name. Add days to the king's life; may his years
span many generations. May he sit enthroned before God forever;
appoint faithful love and truth to guard him. Then I will continually
sing of Your name, fulfilling my vows day by day.*

PSALM 61:5-8

The greatest use of life is to spend it for something that will outlast it.
WILLIAM JAMES

Depending on to whom you're talking at the time, con-
versations about the King will likely invoke numerous
topics. When it comes to rock and roll, there's no doubt
that immortalized crooner Elvis Presley fits the bill. Then
you have the King of Pop, a nickname commonly given to
iconic entertainer Michael Jackson.

History has also provided us with numerous real-life
kings, including such notable biblical leaders as King
David and King Solomon and such well-known English

rulers as King James I (known for his commissioning of the *King James Version* of the Bible) and King Henry VIII (infamously known for his many wives).

But within the world of sports, only one image comes to mind when that nickname is uttered: NASCAR legend Richard Petty.

At six foot two and with the help of his trademark black cowboy hat and boots, Petty towers over most everyone in the garage and can seemingly be seen from half a mile away as he stops to sign autographs for anyone and everyone. His smile, shaded by that recognizable jet-black moustache, is welcoming and sincere. Even though his eyes are hidden by sunglasses, you still get the sense that they are locked in and fully engaged on each and every racing fan who simply wants to get close to greatness.

Robbie Loomis, vice president of Petty Enterprises, remembers the first time he met the King. At the time, he was working as an engineer with Petty's son, Kyle. (Loomis would eventually spend 11 years at Petty Enterprises before moving on to Hendrick Motor Sports as the crew chief for Jeff Gordon and then returning to the Pettys in 2006.)

"It was a little bit intimidating," Loomis recalls. "He looked like he was about 10 feet tall. But he's such a humble, unassuming and caring person. He really makes you feel comfortable in any setting."

Kyle Petty jokes that everyone in the shop—himself included—calls Richard the King as well. It's become a matter of habit for most who simply respect the man for his years of excellence, although Richard Petty still seems a bit uncomfortable with the moniker.

"I don't pay any attention to it," Richard Petty says. "My name's Richard. I've done my thing. I tell them a lot of times, 'It's better to be known as that than some of the stuff people would really like to call you.' They're always calling somebody something."

Richard Petty might have had his fair share of enemies while he was dominating NASCAR throughout the '60s, '70s and '80s, but you wouldn't know that now. Any animosity his opponents once harbored has long since been replaced with praise for the King and his astounding accomplishments.

In a 35-year stock-car racing career that spanned five decades, Petty ran 1,184 races and claimed a record 200 wins, seven Daytona 500 victories and seven NASCAR Cup titles, a feat that only the late Dale Earnhardt Sr. managed to equal.

Richard Petty was preceded by his father, Lee Petty, who was one of the sport's original stars. In just 16 years, Lee Petty won 54 races and three NASCAR titles (an award that at that time was referred to as the Grand National Championship). Lee Petty also founded Petty Enterprises in 1949—an organization that Richard and Kyle still run today.

NASCAR driver Jeff Green drove the #43 car for the Pettys from 2003 to 2005 and was honored to be part of the legendary team. "There's definitely a lot of heritage there," Green says. "Without Richard and Lee and the whole Petty organization, I don't think our sport would be the same. They laid the foundation. As our sport got bigger and better, it's changed a lot; but without those 200 victories and the 43 car and however many victories Lee had, I don't think it would be the same sport."

The legacy of excellence that was started by Lee Petty continued with Richard, whose philosophy on the subject is much like the way he raced and the way he continues to do business: straightforward and simple.

"When you get up in the morning, [you ask], *Can I do a little better than I did yesterday?*" he explains. "That's the challenge of not just staying the same. Can we make our business a little bit better? Can we help somebody today who we didn't help yesterday? It's just life."

Richard Petty has likewise passed on that desire to be the best to his son, Kyle, who has been racing in NASCAR's Cup series since 1979. More importantly, he has made a lasting impression on everyone involved in the sport.

"The names Petty and NASCAR go hand in hand," Nationwide Series driver Jason Keller says. "I don't think you can think of one without the other really. Richard Petty has done so much for the sport, and Kyle has followed in those footsteps. I've been fortunate enough to do some autograph sessions with Kyle, and it's just amazing how the fans relate to him and how personable he is with the fans. He's no different with the fans than he is with us drivers. I think that's what makes him so real—that he's so personable and you can really relate to him."

Tim Griffin, Motor Racing Outreach's lead Sprint Cup chaplain, has also been impressed by the Petty family and their contributions to stock-car racing. He often refers to them as "the class of NASCAR," not just because of their commitment to excellence on the track, but also because of how they serve the needs of so many away from the track.

"They're ambassadors of NASCAR," Griffin says. "That's probably the best term for them. They're the class, the standard, both on and off the track. Their desire to elevate the sport with class and dignity is really unparalleled. They've been at it for so long, and they've gained such a high level of professionalism and created so much respect from the community itself. You can't help but respect that."

Kyle Petty has benefited from seeing his father in action as far back as he can remember. He raced for Petty Enterprises from 1979 to 1984 and—following stints with the Wood Brothers and Felix Sabates's Sabco Racing—has been back with the organization since 1997.

Whether it was hanging out in the garage area as an eight-year-old kid or riding in cars owned by his father, Kyle Petty has learned a great deal about excellence, including a personal definition that has taken years of firsthand experience and secondhand observation to craft.

"For me, excellence means always striving to do one's best," he says. "It's pushing past your comfort zone sometimes—not necessarily meeting others' expectations, but meeting God's expectations."

Kyle Petty has wisely taken the advice found in Job 8:8-9, which says, "For ask the previous generation, and pay attention to what their fathers discovered, since we were [born only] yesterday and know nothing. Our days on earth are but a shadow."

To that end, Petty says he has gleaned many amazing nuggets of wisdom from watching his father in action.

"I've learned to always take the high road," Kyle says. "I've learned to know that God will always serve your needs, even when you aren't sure what your needs may be. He is there. He is with you and helping to guide you to make the right decisions in all aspects of your life. There have certainly been times when we have questioned things that have happened in our lives, but we know that God's strength and power are at work."

In essence, it is the Pettys' faith that is at the crux of their pursuit of excellence. Richard Petty cites his wife, Lynda, as the key to his family's commitment to God, while Kyle Petty mentions his Grandmothers Petty and Owens for laying the foundation of faith.

"I don't think you can take your faith in God and put it in a pigeonhole," Kyle says. "It's there all the time, every day, everywhere you're at. It's not something that you put in your pocket, and you bring it out to show people and then put it back up. It's not like a new watch. You need to have it all the time. It shows in not only what you do and how you do it, but how you lead your entire life and not just the time you get to stand in front of a TV camera for 32 seconds on a Sunday afternoon. That's the time that people see you, and that's the time you use for witnessing. That's a good thing to be able to use.

"But at the same time, it's just as important for that guy that you stop to talk to on the side of the road or someone you're having dinner with and talking one on one," he adds. "You may reach just as many people."

As a testament to his strong faith, Kyle Petty has been a longtime supporter of Motor Racing Outreach, and Tim Griffin always enjoys his weekend visits with Petty—whether it be at Sunday morning chapel service, prerace prayer time or just a random encounter.

"Before the race, we have the privilege of going to each team as they're on the starting grid before they climb into their car and go out to race," Griffin says. "We pray with each driver. At Michigan one year, I remember Kyle said to me, 'You know, the reason I come to chapel is that I just want to hear the Word. That's what I'm here for. That's what most interests me.'"

In 2000, the Petty family's faith was tested profoundly. On April 5, Lee Petty passed away at the age of 86 after complications from surgery for a stomach aneurysm. While losing a father, grandfather and great-grandfather was difficult, nothing could prepare the Pettys for the tragedy of

May 12. On that day, Kyle Petty's oldest son, Adam, was taking practice laps for the Busch (now Nationwide) Series race at the New Hampshire International Speedway when the throttle in his car stuck and caused him to hit the wall head-on. He was killed instantly.

Adam Petty's death sent shockwaves throughout NASCAR, not just because he was a fellow driver, but also because he had become a part of the family. His grandfather Richard Petty says that all of the veteran drivers had known him since he was a child and had adopted him as one of their own.

"When something like that happens, it doesn't only happen to your family, it happens to this entire community," Kyle Petty explains. "This is a community. That's what you've got to keep in mind as well. When you talk about this sport, you've got to remember that we're going to go over there, we're all going to work on our cars, we're all going to go out there on the racetrack and try to beat each other's head in. But after all that's over, we'll come right back over here and, look, we're neighbors with each other."

Prior to his death, Adam Petty had shown great interest in camps that cater to kids with special physical needs and had expressed a desire to help build one near the family headquarters in Level Cross, North Carolina. So when he was tragically lost at the age of 19, Kyle and his wife, Pattie, decided to fulfill their son's dream.

The result was Victory Junction Gang Camp, which

focuses on children with chronic and life-threatening diseases. Richard Petty donated 70 acres of land, and this was followed by donations from many others, including fellow drivers Dale Jarrett, Bobby Labonte, Tony Stewart, Kevin Harvick, Michael Waltrip, Kurt Busch, Jeff Gordon and Jimmie Johnson, just to name a few.

Built to look like key elements of a racetrack, the medically safe camp is a place where kids can enjoy simple pleasures such as swimming, bowling and fishing—things that their conditions would otherwise prevent them from doing. Kyle Petty and his family are constantly raising money to ensure that all campers can attend the camp at no cost.

Victory Junction Gang Camp has become one of the Pettys' great passions. Some have even commented that helping hundreds of kids every year has overtaken the family's desire to win races, although few (if any) would suggest that the competitive fire at Petty Enterprises has been extinguished. But there is a greater realization from Richard and Kyle that their legacy of excellence is wrapped up in much more than fortune and fame. Instead, they can turn to the Bible for examples of what such a legacy should look like. Proverbs 13:22, for instance, tells us that "a good man leaves an inheritance to his grandchildren, but the sinner's wealth is stored up for the righteous."

"To be excellent at what you do is a result of faith," Kyle Petty explains. "Ultimately, we are God's children and are here to serve as disciples of Christ. Always striving for excellence sometimes means foregoing the immediate benefits in exchange for long term."

That sobering thought also brings to mind one of David's prayers found in Psalm 61:5-8:

> God, You have heard my vows; You have given a heritage to those who fear Your name. Add days to the king's life; may his years span many generations. May he sit enthroned before God forever; appoint faithful love and truth to guard him. Then I will continually sing of Your name, fulfilling my vows day by day.

While Richard Petty is already experiencing some of this passage's promise, he rarely stops to think about the legacy of excellence through a lifetime of serving and integrity that he is actively creating for his family and the NASCAR community.

"I haven't really ever gone there," Richard says. "We're doing our thing in our time under our circumstances. Hopefully, you leave a good taste in everybody's mouth, and they remember the good. If something happened to us right now and we're not here anymore, we would hope that you would forget about the racing part and go to the camp, the things that we have left that will enrich other people's lives later down the road where racing won't. Racing will be history and that's what we happened to do, but [the camp] is what we left for the rest of the world."

Kyle Petty wholeheartedly agrees with his father's wise words and has similar thoughts on the subject of legacy. "You're only here 60, 70, 80, 100 years—whatever it is," he says. "In the big picture, you're not here that long. I don't think you need to worry about your legacy. But how do you know that your legacy's not that some kid who has spina bifida or has hemophilia or has AIDS comes to camp and at some point in time 20 or 30 years from now, he has a son or a daughter and tells them about a camp he went to when he was young and then this child grows up and discovers a cure for cancer?"

Tim Griffin has seen the Pettys forge ahead in their quest for excellence and can't help but be inspired by their impeccable vision and unshakable resolve.

"You can't worry about your legacy," he concurs. "It can't be part of your goal. It's a by-product of doing the right thing today. The Pettys have grown to understand that it's an improper focus to have your mind fixed on what people are going to think about you. You've just got to do the right thing that's in front of you today."

As a follower of Christ, Kyle Petty is driven to excellence and understands its ultimate purpose in the grand scheme of life.

"That's simple," he says. "I want to please God. I want Him to know that I believe in Him as my Savior, and because of that, I will do all things to please Him. He has played a large part in my family's life. We are here because of Him. Sure, we question why some things have happened and always will. But it is because of faith that we can pick up and move forward, using those experiences to make us stronger followers of Christ and to strive for excellence in all that we do."

TRAINING TIME

1. If there were a poll taken among your family, friends and acquaintances, what do you think most people would say is the most unique thing about you? For what qualities would you like to be remembered?

2. Kyle Petty says that excellence is "meeting God's expectations." What do you think are some of God's expectations for your life? What part does excellence play in your legacy?

3. Read Job 8:8-9. How often do you ask for advice from others? As you strive for excellence, what can you gain by following the admonition found in Job 8:8-9? How has paying attention to "the previous generation" taught you a valuable lesson about athletics or life in general?

4. Read Proverbs 13:22. What are some examples of "an inheritance" that someone could leave to his or her children and grandchildren? What kind of inheritance or treasure (whether physical or spiritual) do you hope to leave those who follow in your footsteps?

5. Read Psalm 61:5-8. What does David suggest are some key elements to a godly legacy? What are some of the blessings that accompany that kind of lifestyle? How does having the wrong focus (worrying about what others think of you) hinder your legacy?

"My grandmother Petty went to a Methodist church in Level Cross and my grandmother Owens went to a Methodist church in Randleman. My mom always had something going at the church or at the school. She worked for the PTA. She was a Scout teacher. She was in 4-H. She and my grandmothers were always doing something. We grew up in small communities, and the churches are the hearts of small communities. I don't care how you look at it. I know that the first President [Bush] and President George W. Bush talked about faith-based initiatives, but faith-based initiatives start in rural America. When somebody's house burns down, the church is the first one there to try to do something. The church has the covered-dish suppers to raise money for a family who's lost something or had a tragedy. That's faith in action. Do unto others as you would have them do unto you. That's it. Everything sprouts from that. [Faith] has an important place in this sport. Even though the demographics continue to change, this is still a grassroots, blue-collar sport. America is still basically a blue-collar nation and a grassroots working-man's nation. And when you go there and you talk to those people, what's the center of their life? The center of their life is Wednesday-night prayer meeting and Sunday-morning church service and Sunday School, and then they'll go watch a race or watch football. God and church always comes first."

—Kyle Petty

8

GOING THE DISTANCE

Ryan Hall
Olympic Marathon Runner

Though a righteous man falls seven times, he will get up, but the
wicked will stumble into ruin.

PROVERBS 24:16

Nothing in this world can take the place of persistence. Talent will
not; nothing is more common than unsuccessful people with talent.
Genius will not; unrewarded genius is almost a proverb. Education
will not; the world is full of educated derelicts. Persistence and
determination alone are omnipotent. The slogan "press on" has
solved and always will solve the problems of the human race.

CALVIN COOLIDGE

To hear Ryan Hall nonchalantly describe his winding
journey as a long-distance runner isn't much different
from watching him glide with apparent ease through
treacherous hills and valleys en route to the finish line.
But just because he makes it look effortless doesn't mean
his path to competitive greatness has been without a fair
number of trials and tribulations.

"I've had a really rocky journey," Hall says. "The hardest thing is picking yourself up after a shattered dream or an injury or when you know you didn't give your best."

Born in Kirkland, Washington, and a resident of Big Bear Lake, California, since the age of five, Hall first became interested in running when he was in the eighth grade. He grew up in a Christian home as the third of five children. But even though his parents did their best to instill godly principles into his life, he admits heading the wrong way as a teenager while pursuing traditional sports such as baseball, basketball and football—a lifestyle that found him in the middle of the cool crowd and an increasingly active party scene.

"We were young, so we weren't into drinking and drugs, but it was heading that direction," Hall says. "But when I started running, my lifestyle changed a lot. I lost a lot of those friends. So I was around a whole different group of people. That put me out of the cool group. I remember just feeling a void at that point and a little bit lonely. Socially I wasn't fitting in anymore. I was kind of struggling with that. Jesus really became my best friend at that point. When I was feeling that void, I would go to Him for that relationship that I was looking for and that was the real beginning of my walk with Christ—and it's been growing ever since."

Hall's development as a long-distance runner was slow and steady, but by his junior year, the hard work finally began to pay off. He claimed the California State cross country title as a junior and senior and won state titles in the two-mile as a junior and in the 1600-meter as a senior. Hall also finished third at the Footlocker Nationals in Orlando.

That success drew the attention of Stanford University, home of one of the nation's premier cross country and track programs. After a solid freshman year, Hall's next two seasons at Stanford were hindered by injuries. Discouraged by his physical health and overall performance up to that point, he decided that he needed to rethink his priorities and took a leave of absence from the team.

"I went through a really rough patch during my sophomore year at Stanford where I actually went home for a quarter and needed to just figure out if that's where God called me to be," Hall says. "I was really questioning whether He wanted me there or not. I was struggling with my identity. While I was a Christian and my faith was really important to me, my worth was coming from my athletic performances. If I wasn't running well, I didn't have a good view of myself. I had to go back home and figure out where I was supposed to be and my identity and my value. That's when I really made the shift."

With a renewed sense of purpose, Hall returned to Stanford and led his team to the 2003 NCAA Cross-Country Championship with a second-place finish, and he was named All-American for a second straight season. As a senior, he won the pre-nationals in Terre Haute, Indiana, and won the 5000-meter title at the NCAA track and field championships. Following his collegiate career, Hall continued to compete professionally, including a successful European stint in 2006. Although he had tinkered with longer distances before, it wasn't until he returned home from Europe that he started to consider making the switch from the middle distances in which he had excelled to marathon distances.

"With the Olympics around the corner, I was trying to figure out what I was best suited to run," Hall says. "Then I took a good, honest look at myself and realized I probably wasn't going to develop a whole lot more in terms of speed. I was trying to figure out how God made me and what event best suits me. That's when I turned my attention to the marathon."

Ironically, Hall remembers a time when even the 10K was an unpleasant chore. After running the event at the cross-country nationals his sophomore year at Stanford, he told his father how much he hated the distance and didn't want to run it again. "That's because I wasn't strong enough, and I didn't have enough endurance for that race," Hall explains. "It's funny that I'm doing marathons now. I would have never thought I would run marathons at this young of an age. I didn't see it as my premier event growing up and through college. That's just a good example of how we're able to grow more than we think or could imagine in the area of endurance when we challenge ourselves."

Hall says there has been a stereotype within the U.S. that the marathon is something runners do at the end of their career, when they are no longer competitive on the track. Long gone are the days of Alberto Salazar and Frank Shorter. But Hall says he is part of a burgeoning movement among younger competitors looking to put the event back on the map here in America.

Hall took a huge leap in accomplishing that goal with his very first marathon on April 22, 2007—the Flora London Marathon—where he finished seventh in a time of 2:08:24 and set a record for American-born citizens. In his second marathon on November 3, 2007, he qualified for the 2008 U.S. Olympic team by winning the Team Trials. He followed that up on April 13, 2008, at the Flora London Marathon by breaking his own American-born record with a fifth-place finish in a time of 2:06:17. At the 2008 Summer Olympics in Beijing, China, Hall finished an impressive tenth place amid the world's elite marathoners.

Throughout his career, Hall has found inspiration in a friendship with legendary runner Jim Ryun and his family. He is also a big fan of Scottish Olympian Eric Liddell, whose story was told in the film *Chariots of Fire*. But Hall's greatest source of strength comes from God's Word. One of his favorite passages is 2 Chronicles 16:9, which says, "For the eyes of the Lord move to and fro throughout the earth that He may strongly support those whose heart is completely His" (*NASB*). "That verse challenges me like no other verse in the Bible," Hall says. "It's asking where my heart is at every moment of every day. Is my heart completely His? That's what I'm striving for in my daily life."

As Hall's relationship with Jesus has grown, so has his understanding of excellence. Part of his early struggles as a runner were based on the identity crisis that often takes place for those sports competitors who have highly measurable templates for success.

"The world's definition of excellence is just based on performance," Hall says. "As soon as you're not performing, no one wants to talk to you anymore in the media, and it's easy to get down on yourself. It's all wrapped up in performance. It's like building your house on the sand. It's very changing and fleeting, and eventually it's going to be gone, because no one is always on top of their game.

"But when you find your identity in Christ and in what He's done for you, it's the unchanging, sturdy rock that you can always stand on," he continues. "You can have a much healthier perspective on yourself and in life in general and in where your hope lies. When I'm not performing well, I lose my hope. I lose my joy. I get down. I get depressed. But when you find your identity in Christ, that's unchanging. No matter what you do, you can't mess that up."

Another one of Hall's favorite Bible verses is found in the commonly quoted Philippians 4:13: "I am able to do all things through Him who strengthens me." But instead of resting solely on that promise, he prefers to back it up with Philippians 4:12—a lesser-known Scripture that adds greater context: "I know both how to have a little, and I know how to have a lot. In any and all circumstances I have learned the secret [of being content]—whether well-fed or hungry, whether in abundance or in need."

For Hall, the aspect of contentment is a foundational key to excellence, because it opens the door to endurance and a never-give-up attitude. "After my performance in London, I was on a huge high; and then I took a break, and I came back and started my training again—and all of the sudden I'm back at ground zero," Hall says. "At that point, I was unfit, and it's not fun to be unfit. I'm used to feeling really good and I'm used to just flying along; but when I start back up after taking some time off, I'm sluggish and not very fit, and it's easy to get negative and unthankful. That verse inspires me to have that attitude of gratitude, which is so important for enduring life, enduring hard patches of racing, enduring a hard season where things don't pan out the way you want."

According to Hall, an unthankful heart is just one of many hindrances to endurance and, therefore, excellence. Others that he has personally faced include doubt and unbelief. He also cites the body as an obstacle to endurance—especially for those who struggle with physical discipline. But for all of these challenges, Hall relies unequivocally on his relationship with God.

"The Bible is the best sports psychology in the world," he says. "It's truth and it applies to every aspect of our lives. The more grounded I am in that and the more truth I have flowing in me, the less often I lose hope and get down and go through those tough times."

Of course, applying these principles to one's life requires a great amount of discipline in all areas of life—training, nutrition, mental toughness and spiritual upkeep. It also requires something else that is often overlooked but will nonetheless make or break any athlete: rest and recovery. Hall, for instance, trains hard for three months and then backs off the last three weeks leading up to a race.

"That's huge," he says. "When you look at things in cycles, there is a season for everything. There have been times when I was at the end of the season and I was really excited about the way things had gone, so I just kept going and didn't take a break. That would totally come back to bite me."

Hall equates an athlete's need for rest and recovery to the Old Testament principle of land conservation through furloughs. In Leviticus 25:2-4, God tells the Israelites to plant and harvest their fields and vineyards for six years but then to rest the land in the seventh year as "a Sabbath to the LORD." The rest and recovery phase of endurance was confirmed by Jesus in Matthew 11:28, where He says, "Come to Me, all of you who are weary and burdened, and I will give you rest."

"That just seems like a principle that God has set since the beginning of time when He took a break on the seventh day," Hall says. "Our bodies are just geared toward work and then recovery. You can't skimp on that recovery time; otherwise, your body won't adapt to the next cycle of training. It's easy to want to leave that part out, because you get the mentality that you just want to work harder and harder, but recovery is definitely an important part of training."

Hall believes that everything he does as a long-distance runner can and should be connected to his spiritual life. He believes that work and worship need to be interwoven—a concept advocated by Brother Lawrence, a seventeenth-century Carmelite monk whose life Hall has studied. "You have to make a point to get into God's Word—even if it's just a little bit every day," Hall says. "I also do my best to pray without ceasing [as instructed in 1 Thessalonians 5:17]. That's a very challenging Scripture for me. But I've been very inspired by Brother Lawrence. It didn't matter what he was doing—if he was doing the dishes or whatever—he could always be praying. So I've tried to take those quiet moments and make them times of prayer."

Ultimately, endurance for Hall—both physically and spiritually speaking—is all about picking himself up. As a kid, he always pondered what it would take to be an Olympian. Now that he has achieved that lofty goal, he remains humbled by the responsibility attached to such a title. "It's not like I feel like I'm so great or that I've done anything that special to deserve to get to the Olympics," Hall says. "I feel like the thing I've done best is that I've just gotten back up from all of the licking I've taken, both physically and spiritually. I'm a pretty black-and-white person. I'll try to live the best I can; and then I'll mess up and fall, and I'll get all down and upset with myself. I've learned over the years not to let myself get as emotionally down when I mess up, and I try to pick myself up off the ground quicker after making a mistake."

Throughout the process, Hall has clung to the encouraging message found in Proverbs 24:16: "Though a righteous man falls seven times, he will get up, but the wicked will stumble into ruin." "I love that verse," Hall says. "It really inspires me because I feel like it summarizes a lot of my physical and spiritual journeys to this point. I'm definitely not perfect by any stretch."

Hall admits that the quest for godly excellence can seem overwhelming at times. But one thing he has come to understand as truth is the fact that excellence cannot exist without endurance and that endurance can only come through a relationship with Christ.

"Seeking God at a young age is so important," Hall says. "When I was 14 years old, I got this idea to run around the lake in my hometown. It was almost like God was whispering that into my ear. And because I decided to obey that and give it a shot, here I am an Olympian and I'm a professional athlete, and I'm doing what I feel like God has made me to do.

"A big part of starting out on your path to excellence is figuring out what God has called you to do and how He's made you and then making those decisions to follow that calling in your life at a young age," Hall concludes. "It really changes the whole trajectory of your life."

TRAINING TIME

1. What are some one-word labels that your friends, teammates or coworkers would use to describe what you are all about? Of those labels, which ones would you rank as the most important? The least important? What are some hidden abilities or characteristics that you would like others to recognize in you?

2. Read 2 Chronicles 16:9. When God's eyes fall on you, what do you think He sees in your heart? How would finding your identity in Christ change your motives for excellence?

3. Read Philippians 4:12-13. How does an attitude of contentment give strength to those striving for excellence? How do you think verse 12 relates to the inspirational truth found in verse 13?

4. Read Leviticus 25:2-4. How can this passage in Leviticus apply to both our physical and spiritual training? When did a time of rest allow you to push forward and be successful in competition?

5. Read Proverbs 24:16. Hall believes that the key to endurance is not getting emotionally down after making a mistake. How does this passage in Proverbs inspire you to never give up? Describe a time when you stumbled or failed but chose to continue. Where did you find the courage to do so?

"Before all of my big races, I like to watch *The Passion of the Christ*, because that's an amazing picture of how Christ endured so much for us. I think about His motivation and what it must have been like for Him to endure that type of pain for that long of a time. It makes me feel that what I do isn't that big of a deal in comparison. I think about His motivation and how He was thinking about other people. Sometimes I can be a very selfish runner, so I try to think about others more when I'm running. That helps me endure more than I could endure if I was just doing it for myself. So obviously I think about the Lord when I'm out there running. I think about Him taking that cross up to Calvary. I also think about other people who I love. I think about my wife when I'm out there running. I think about the kids in Africa who we're helping through World Vision. Thinking about doing things for others rather than making a selfish endeavor really brings so much more meaning to my running and helps me to endure through those tough times. The Bible says that Christ endured the cross for the joy set before Him. There's a prize waiting for us at the end that we can fix our eyes on. It will allow us to endure things that we never thought we could possibly go through."

—Ryan Hall

9

No Pain, No Gain

Chris Byrd
Former Heavyweight Boxing Champion

I do not run like one who runs aimlessly, or box like one who beats the air. Instead, I discipline my body and bring it under strict control, so that after preaching to others, I myself will not be disqualified.

1 CORINTHIANS 9:26-27

Some people have greatness thrust upon them. Few have excellence thrust upon them. . . . They achieve it. They do not achieve it unwittingly by doing what comes naturally and they don't stumble into it in the course of amusing themselves. All excellence involves discipline and tenacity of purpose.

JOHN W. GARDNER

When Chris Byrd hears the iconic pop-culture phrase "What happens in Vegas stays in Vegas," he can't help but crack a smile. And not for the reasons you would assume, coming from the former World Boxing Organization (WBO) and International Boxing Federation (IBF) heavyweight champion who also happens to reside in Nevada's self-proclaimed Sin City.

"For me, I put Christ first," Byrd says. "I still do the same things I've always done. I stay home when I'm training, so I can be in church and not in some secluded place. I want to live my life like I live every day. I'm a boring guy. I don't do anything. I don't know what happens in Vegas. I don't know anything about this city."

Boxers are among the most disciplined athletes, and Byrd is certainly no exception. Despite the vast array of entertainment options that the Vegas strip so readily offers, he has somehow managed to shield himself from all distractions. His ability to stay focused has been a work in progress that dates back to his early days growing up in Flint, Michigan.

Byrd's foray into athletic competition began at the age of 5, and by the time he was 10, he was fully immersed in an amateur boxing career. His father, Joe Byrd Sr., was and still is his trainer and is also known as one of the finest "cut men" in the professional boxing ranks. His mother, Rose Byrd, was also a part of the process and one (if not both) of his parents can usually be found in his corner on fight night.

"My parents pushed me to a whole other level my entire life," Byrd says. "They wanted nothing but great things from their kids. It goes back to the training part. When my mother's in the corner with me, she's always whispering in my ear, 'You know how hard you worked. You remember all those miles you ran. You remember all the stuff you went through.' She made me into a beast in the ring. It's crazy. She made me really tough. She wanted excellence from every one of her kids because of how hard we trained. My parents never settled for anything less than excellence."

By the age of 23, Byrd had racked up 275 amateur wins and had claimed three U.S. amateur titles (1989, 1991 and 1992). As a middleweight, he won the silver medal at the 1992 Summer Olympics in Barcelona, Spain, and won the gold medal at the 1992 Canada Cup.

Everything in Byrd's life was seemingly perfect. He was married to his high-school sweetheart, Tracy, and was the proud father of daughter Jordan (two more children—son Justin and daughter Sydney—were added to the family later on). But the one key element that Byrd lacked was a relationship with God. So when Tracy began taking Jordan to church, Byrd curiously took notice. Then, when his wife later gave her heart to Christ, his interest was really piqued—although not necessarily in a positive way.

"She got saved and I was like, 'Wow, what's that?'" Byrd says. "'I'm not going in that direction because I don't want to be like that.' My brother and sister-and-law had gotten saved five years earlier, and I thought they were strange, so I didn't want to be like that."

As his wife and daughter continued their spiritual walk, Byrd quickly started to feel left out. Begrudgingly, he opted to tag along and, eventually, had a miraculous change of heart.

"I went a few weeks and really wasn't listening," Byrd says. "But one week I listened, and God just convicted my heart so bad. I truly understood why Christ died for me. I walked that aisle, and someone led me to the Lord."

By then, Byrd was embarking on his professional boxing career and was still fighting as a svelte 175-pound middleweight. But after three fights, he felt inspired to move all the way up to the heavyweight division. Byrd was so convinced that this move was part of God's plan, he prayed for supernatural intervention.

"I can honestly tell you that I spoke to the Lord," Byrd says. "I wanted to be a heavyweight. I was tired of losing the weight, and my career at that time was going nowhere. There were no major guys in the division. I told the Lord, 'If I can be a heavyweight, I will be a witness for You. I won't forget about You. . . . It's going to be all about You.'"

God answered his prayer, and almost immediately Byrd began to gain weight until he was a rock-solid 210 pounds. In April 2000, the six-foot-one fighter defeated Vitali Klitschko in Berlin, Germany, for the WBO title. Byrd lost that belt six months later, but in December 2002, he claimed the IBF title by defeating Evander Holyfield.

After his career-altering victory over Holyfield, Byrd seemed to be on top of the boxing world, but he was fighting another kind of battle internally. "I won't say I was playing the Christian game, but as far as boxing was concerned, it was still all about me," Byrd says. "After I beat

Holyfield, no other heavyweight wanted to fight me because my style was too hard. It was like that for a long time. I was on top of the world. And the guy came over to my house and did an interview; and then *Sports Illustrated* said I was the baddest man on the planet, and it was like, 'Wow.' It was that inward pride. I thought it was all about me."

In September 2003, Byrd stepped into the ring for his first title defense against Fres Oquendo. The fight was originally supposed to be a co-main event on HBO, but then the network decided to focus only on Byrd's fight as the featured bout.

"That took me over the top," Byrd recalls. "I thought, *I am the man. This is all about me.* But the fight with Oquendo was a horrible fight. The only way it could've gone worse is if I would've lost. But it was really like a loss. It was controversial. People thought I lost. I got all of these bad emails. After the fight, I stayed in my house for about two weeks. I don't even think I went to church. I was so embarrassed. The Lord put me in my place."

Byrd had learned the hard truth found in Proverbs 16:18: "Pride comes before destruction, and an arrogant spirit before a fall." After that humbling experience, Byrd prayed for forgiveness and vowed to never let selfishness and ego get in the way of what God had called him to do.

Although Byrd eventually lost his IBF title to Wladamir Klitschko in 2006 and lost to Alexander Povetkin in 2007 as part of the IBF heavyweight tournament, Byrd still found ways to use his platform to share God's love with others. Both losses took place in Germany, where his demeanor and strong moral character made a lasting impression on the nation's rabid boxing fans.

Byrd then decided to drop down to the light heavyweight division in an effort to revitalize his career. And though Byrd lost in his first light heavyweight fight against Shaun George (and ultimately retired from the sport shortly following the May 2008 bout), he maintains a deeper revelation of his purpose as a boxer and as a follower of Christ. To that end, his pursuit of excellence on all fronts has taken on greater significance. Just as before, it still comes down to preparation, but Byrd's full surrender and trust in God for the results—win or lose—gives his legendary work ethic new meaning.

"I know I'm going to be excellent in my sport because I'm good at what I do," Byrd says. "But if my training is perfect, if I do everything in order, I'm going to achieve the goal that God has put in front of me. If you give it your all and you know you've got the ability to be the best and you achieve that, there's nothing better. And you bring glory to God by doing it. That's excellence."

When Byrd isn't training for a fight, he still maintains an extremely disciplined routine. But five weeks leading up to any given bout, things get intense, although his methods are quite a bit different from the average professional boxer. "Most guys go to training camp," Byrd says. "So they're off somewhere in high altitudes up in the mountains or they're in seclusion. I'm at home. I've always

115

been at home. It never changes. I get up early—4:30 or 5 o'clock in the morning—and run my miles. I'll come back and eat a small meal and try to get some liquid in me; then I lift weights and then I'm off to the gym."

Following this routine has taught Byrd the truth of a popular cliché from the 1980s: "No pain, no gain." The less catchy phrase in its original form can be found in Hebrews 12:11: "No discipline seems pleasant at the time, but painful. Later on, however, it produces a harvest of righteousness and peace for those who have been trained by it" (*NIV*).

"Hard work is everything," Byrd says. "Hard work will bring excellence—even in losing. If a guy beats me, he was just better than me, but I know I did everything I could. I was in great shape. So I'm going to get excellence out of what I do."

Thanks to his experiences in Germany, Byrd can also attest to another biblical truth tied to the concept of excellence: Self-control for the believer is more beneficial than self-control for the nonbeliever (see 1 Corinthians 9:25-27). The reason for this is because Christians who exercise self-control do so in order to receive an "imperishable" crown, or, in other words, benefits that will carry over into their eternal life.

Paul goes on to describe one who only trains with discipline as an athlete who runs "aimlessly, or box like one who beats the air." But for the follower of Christ, self-control affords the opportunity to speak into others' lives and keeps us from being "disqualified" because of a hypocritical lifestyle.

Byrd believes that many challenges to discipline and self-control exist. He personally has to be careful about his diet in order to stay in top physical condition during training and during his fights. Byrd has also observed that many in his profession have specific struggles with relationships that often cause them trouble, often losing years from their careers.

"I came out of the Olympics and started getting notoriety," Byrd says. "Then I moved up to the heavyweight division and started getting more fame on top of that. It really could have gone to my head.... You've got to stay on point because if you're a good athlete, it will mess you up."

Byrd again takes his cue from some key New Testament writings. In this case, the admonition to remain disciplined can be found in Romans 6:12-13:

> Therefore do not let sin reign in your mortal body, so that you obey its desires. And do not offer any parts of it to sin as weapons for unrighteousness. But as those who are alive from the dead, offer yourselves to God, and all the parts of yourselves to God as weapons for righteousness.

While some believers might question the violent nature of Byrd's sport, it's apparent that his body (and more specifically, his hands) has quite literally become a

117

"[weapon] for righteousness." And that quest for excellence doesn't just end in the ring. It carries over into every facet of his life.

"I want to be the best," Byrd says. "I want to be the perfect husband for my wife. It's not so I can brag. I just want her to feel so comfortable and so proud of the fact that she can trust everything her husband does. I want to be an excellent father. I want my kids to be proud of me. And I'm really stern. I'm not a pushover. But at the same time I'm really fair, and they know I love them. I try to live according to what the Bible says. I'm not perfect. I just try to be a godly father."

Byrd is a blessed man, just as all who claim Christ as Savior are blessed. That's why he believes firmly Jesus' words in Luke 12:48: "Much will be required of everyone who has been given much. And even more will be expected of the one who has been entrusted with more."

"God is expecting more from us as Christians," Byrd says. "He wants us to put our faith in Him and know that we trust Him and know that He is able to do it. All you have to do is look at the Israelites. They never trusted Him for anything; and when they did, it was only for that time, and then they'd soon forget what God had done for them. The Lord has brought me out of Egypt and he's brought me through the wilderness. I'm not going to stay in the wilderness when I probably only have 40 miles to go."

Byrd certainly experienced times in the wilderness and times in the Promised Land. But the constant that remains for him—as it should for all believers—can be found in 2 Corinthians 8:7, where Paul writes, "Now as you excel in everything—in faith, in speech, in knowledge, in all diligence, and in your love for us—excel also in this grace."

"God wants excellence from you—and not just in sports but in attitude and service," Byrd says. "Have the right attitude. You're representing Him all the time. Let people see Christ through you in your sport. Be a great athlete also. He's given you this ability. Don't cheat yourself. Don't do it halfway. Do it to the fullest because He's in you, and He's expecting more from you. Push yourself to another level. Trust Him for the strength and the endurance to do it.

"As a Christian athlete, I can go that extra mile," Byrd adds. "It's for God's glory."

TRAINING TIME

1. What are some examples of discipline in your sport or field of interest? With which areas of discipline do you tend to struggle? What areas of discipline generally come easier to you?

2. Read 1 Corinthians 9:25-27. What does Paul mean when he says that he doesn't "run like one who runs aimlessly, or box like one who beats the air" (v. 26)? How do you think purpose works together with discipline? Is it possible for your discipline to ultimately have little meaning?

3. Read Romans 6:12-13. What are some things that challenge your physical discipline? What methods do you use to overcome those challenges? What are some things that challenge your spiritual discipline?

4. Read Luke 12:48. What are some things that are required of you as an athlete, student, employee, parent or child? As your level of responsibility increases, how does that impact the decisions you make?

5. What are some things that you have had to sacrifice in your pursuit of excellence? What are some other things that you need to sacrifice in order to fulfill your potential? What are some steps that you need to take in order to maintain a high level of discipline both physically and spiritually?

"When I lost the IBF heavyweight title to Wladimir Klitschko in 2006, it was a down moment for me; but at the same time, it was very impacting. The event was so crazy over in Germany. People were everywhere. I represented Jesus Christ through all of that, and I got so much email from Germans saying, 'We saw your faith in how you lived your life.' They told me they loved my son, Justin, because he went and congratulated Klitschko while he was still crying and upset that I had lost. That's what my boxing is all about—trying to impact people for Christ. Then in 2007, I was back in Germany again to fight Alexander Povetkin in the IBF elimination tournament; and even though I lost, I had another major impact. I was feeling down about losing, but again, who do I do it for? Is it for me or is it to glorify God and get the Word out there? He's using me for that purpose. After the loss, people were coming up to me on the streets to talk to me about the fight. I had to ask my wife, 'Did I win the fight?' Everyone was so positive. Excellence brings glory back to Him. You may not win every time, but your attitude and the way you present yourself—Christ still shines through that. It gives me a chance to witness to people in this perverse and crazy era that we live in."

—Chris Byrd

10

MAKING A MARK

Kay Yow
Head NCAA Women's Basketball Coach

---

*Set an example of good works yourself, with integrity
and dignity in your teaching.*

TITUS 2:7

Example is not the main thing in influencing others, it's the only thing.

ALBERT SCHWEITZER

By most accounts, Kay Yow shouldn't be one of the greatest women's basketball coaches of all time. History alone presents many reasons why her rise to legendary status was improbable at best.

Consider these facts. Yow was born in 1942—a mere 22 years after women gained the right to vote in the United States. When she took her first head girl's basketball coaching job at Allen Jay High School in High Point, North Carolina, in 1964, Title IX—key legislation that opened the door for expanded female participation in sports—was still eight years from passage. And after she took the North Carolina State head coaching job in 1975, another four years would elapse before the creation of the groundbreaking ESPN cable television network, which would eventually make women's basketball a key part of its regular programming.

Still, Yow somehow managed to turn something for which she never planned into one of college basketball's most influential coaching careers, placing her beside such names as John Wooden, Jim Valvano and Pat Summitt.

"This was just something I stumbled into," Yow says. "I know God's hand has been in every part of my life."

Yow's path to greatness began in the rural community of Gibsonville, North Carolina, where there was great support for the school and its sports programs. (Had she been born six miles east in Burlington—a city whose school had no competitive sports for girls—her story might have been very different.) Yow participated in multiple sports at Gibsonville, but when she left for East Carolina University, her athletic career effectively ended due to the lack of women's college teams in the region.

After graduating from ECU, Yow began her teaching career at Allen Jay High School, teaching English. For many years, one man had been coaching both the boys' and the girls' basketball teams at the school, and the school principal asked Yow to take over the girls' team. Although reluctant at first, Yow was finally talked into the coaching position.

Yow spent the next four years at Allen Jay before continuing her education at North Carolina-Greensboro, where she earned her master's in physical education and received her undergraduate certification. After a year at Gibsonville High School, where she coached her youngest sister, Susan, she moved to Elon College (now Elon University), where she served as coordinator of women's athletics, was a full-time professor and coached three sports.

"I had no goal to pursue college coaching," Yow says. "I was really preparing myself to go back to coaching in high school. I had determined that I really loved the field. You work with a smaller number of people, but you just seem to touch them physically, mentally, emotionally, socially and spiritually. You didn't have all of those opportunities by just working in the classroom. It wasn't as powerful as coaching."

In 1975, Yow made the leap to North Carolina State, where she was asked to guide the women's basketball program through its earliest stages. At the same time, she also coached softball and volleyball and coordinated the entire women's athletics department. She led that very first team to the Women's National Invitational Tournament and a 19-7 record.

But something else significant happened to Yow during that first year at NC State. Representatives of Campus Crusade for Christ started to build a relationship with her through weekly visits. A young lady named Lori Moore was especially influential in Yow's life. Her persistence finally caused the head coach to set up a meeting between the ministry and her team.

Although Yow had grown up in church, thanks to the influence of her mother, and says she "felt the nudging of the Holy Spirit many times," she never fully grasped the importance of a personal relationship with Christ.

Yow didn't feel comfortable telling her players that people from Campus Crusade were coming to present the gospel to them, so she decided to devise a compromise that would work for everyone involved. The team would practice only for an hour followed by Moore's 10-minute presentation.

"I was thinking they wouldn't care who was talking for 10 minutes because they were only practicing for one hour," Yow says. "And that's exactly how it worked. So when Lori came, she brought two other girls, and they were very well prepared. They presented the message very clearly and very strongly and boldly."

At the end of the meeting, they passed cards out to the players and coaches with some questions, including one that asked if the person holding the card had prayed the prayer of salvation. Yow felt as if everything had gone well and was glad it was over. But that night around 8 o'clock, she received a call from Moore.

"She was so excited because one person had accepted Christ," Yow recalls. "And she said, 'Of course, you know that was you.' When she presented the gospel message, I was very convicted by the Spirit. I had accepted Jesus as my personal Lord and Savior that day. She was ecstatic and said, 'Coach Yow, if one person would have accepted

Christ today, [I hoped] it would be you . . . because as a leader you can have an impact on so many people.'"

Yow immediately got involved with a local church and was baptized. She also joined forces with NC State's active FCA group and participated in Bible studies. Up to this point, Yow had already committed to the concept of excellence, but her newfound relationship with Christ forced her to rethink her original definition. Now the first thing that comes to her mind is the apostle Paul's inspirational words found in Colossians 3:23: "Whatever you do, do it enthusiastically, as something done for the Lord and not for men."

"Use the talents and abilities that He's given you to honor Him," Yow says. "If that's your motive, I fully know and believe with all my heart that God will guide and direct you and give you the wisdom to have your best chance at excellence. If you do things as unto God rather than unto men and you just give everything from your heart, soul and your mind, you're going to work hard; and working hard is a cornerstone of success. That's just going to come naturally, because you're doing it out of love."

One thing that has remained constant throughout Yow's quest for excellence has been the motivation she has received from successful coaches across the spectrum of athletic competition. She has done well by her mentors—to the tune of 708 career victories and 20 trips to the NCAA tournament through the 2007-08 season. She was the assistant coach on the gold-medal women's basketball team at the 1984 Olympics and was the head coach of the gold-medal team at the 1988 Summer Games. Yow was enshrined in the Women's Basketball Hall of Fame in 2000 and the Naismith Memorial Basketball Hall of Fame in 2002. She was also presented with the inaugural FCA Kay Yow Heart of a Coach award in 2008.

But Yow rarely if ever keeps track of any of those accomplishments. She determined many years ago to live in the moment and press forward to greater levels of excellence. In order to do that, she has keyed in on the word "attitude," which she believes is the secret to successful, excellent living—and nowhere is that better modeled than in the life of Christ. "I love to study Jesus' attitude in all of the situations that He faced and how He responded and how He dealt with things," Yow says. "That's the exciting part for me—to not just try to understand excellence in the field of sports, but in a life guided by Jesus' example. He was an example for what it takes to have excellence. And to me, excellence is all about glorifying God."

For Yow, that means taking on what she considers a serious and sobering responsibility—one she believes should be shared by all who claim to be followers of Jesus. "The scary part is I know that at emotional times, I hope that the truth is strong enough in me and embedded in me that it will come out that way," she candidly admits. "We're human, so there's the problem. I want it to be me. I want it to be who I really am. I don't want to just be doing it because I think that this is what I should be doing.

I want to do it because this is where I am in life. You don't just arrive there suddenly—and you never really arrive. You just keep going deeper and deeper."

Yow has provided an amazing picture of excellence to her players, to the NC State fans and to the sports world at large for reasons that extend well beyond the basketball court. In 1987, she was diagnosed with breast cancer. It went into remission for several years, but it returned in 2004. Yow fought the disease through a combination of medical and natural treatments, but by November 2006 it had progressed to the point where she knew that she had to temporarily step away from the team.

Despite an ongoing battle with cancer, Yow made her way back to the bench after missing only 16 games, and she continues to lead by example and by the power of her words. "You're constantly talking to your players about what they need to do to pursue excellence," Yow says. "As a coach, people see me and think I'm coaching basketball. But I think I'm coaching people. If you become a winner as a person, you will have your best chance to win on the court. You need to develop the characteristics and qualities that give you the best chance at being successful. I think that people without character, they always fall short of excellence. No matter how talented they are or how great a player they are, they will fall short. At the time you need them the most, they will fail you."

That's why Yow so adamantly follows the instruction that Paul gave his young disciple in Titus 2:7: "Set an example of good works yourself, with integrity and dignity in your teaching." "In order to be successful, you must have character," Yow says. "That's what you always teach your players at teachable moments. You teach them about developing greater character that will help them to produce excellence."

There are many Scriptures that describe God as a Father who disciplines His children because He loves them. Yow subscribes to that philosophy, but she is quick to point out the importance of love in the equation—along with an equal measure of truth. "You deal with people by encouraging them," Yow says. "Of course, you have to correct, but there's that saying 'Truth without love is hypocrisy.' You cannot love without truth. You've got to tell the truth to help them move to a higher level. But if you give the truth without love, it becomes very cold.

"What we speak and how we speak comes out of our heart," she adds. "Each of us can let things come out of our mouth and realize that there's a problem. Sometimes when I hear my players say certain things, I'm reminded that out of the heart, the mouth speaks. So you just have to be a role model. You have to be an example. It takes action and it takes attitude. Actions speak louder than words, and attitude speaks louder than actions. You have to live by what you say. That speaks to a person's integrity."

Throughout her legendary coaching career, Yow has witnessed many changes in the makeup of her players. With each passing generation, excellence has become a more-measured quality, whether that's by number of awards, accolades in the press, or display of material wealth. Unfortunately, not everyone who achieves such things can truly lay claim to the mantle of excellence.

"When people think about excellence, a lot of times they're thinking about the end result—the production," Yow claims. "I think they forget about the process and about the journey. This is where all the learning takes place. People don't always see the big picture. They see more of the short term. To so many people, success is just money or position or power or title. Yet if they haven't given their very best and they haven't done it in the way that it should be done—I mean some people step on people to get what they want—then that's not excellence. A commitment to value and doing it the right way is just as important to excellence as anything else."

With society's misunderstanding of what true excellence looks like comes the temptation to take shortcuts to success. Few seem willing to put in the time, effort and disciplined hard work that is necessary. As far as Yow is concerned, however, shortcuts simply cheapen the end result. "Everything in life today is about getting there quickly," she says. "But all things that are worthwhile are worth working for and worth waiting for. We're just going for the wrong things. The price tags are on the wrong things. The price tags need to be on the value and the character. Living successfully with our character and our values beats becoming successful by taking shortcuts."

Yow has yet to discover a shortcut attractive enough to take. Instead, she finds great blessings and rewards in seeing the fruit of her consistent, disciplined approach to coaching and teaching. It's in those moments when Yow can almost literally see the lights turn on in the hearts and minds of her athletes that everything is suddenly worth the effort.

"We get so many awards in athletics, but I've always associated rewards as something that are on the inside," she says. "Awards get tarnished. You lose them. You break them. But rewards are something that you keep forever. I've always treasured the rewards so much more than awards. Seeing your players start to understand the true meaning of excellence is one of those rewards. You know that they've taken a great step forward in life and in understanding how to live successfully and not only to become successful. There's a real distinction for me between living successfully and becoming successful."

But don't ask Yow to get too specific with those personal breakthroughs because, quite frankly, she's too busy living for the here and now to remember them all. And besides, true excellence doesn't keep track of itself—otherwise, it would become something else. Instead, Yow does her best to strive for the kind of excellence displayed by the selfless example of God's Son.

"You living it is much more powerful than you saying it," Yow says. "Jesus lived it. We have His words, but we also have His actions. That's so powerful."

TRAINING TIME

1. Kay Yow has been more than just a great coach. She has been a great teacher. Who are some people who have been influential teachers in your life? What important lessons did you learn through their words and their example?

2. Read Titus 2:7. How can a lifestyle of excellence "set an example" for others? Can you describe a time in your life when you were able to teach others about excellence through your actions?

3. Read Proverbs 3:12 and Revelation 3:19. How important do you think good character and integrity are in leading others to excellence? How easy or difficult is it for you to receive correction, whether it's from a coach, a parent, an employer or a friend?

4. Read Luke 6:39-40. Have you ever been under the leadership of someone who didn't seem to know what he or she was doing? What challenges did that scenario create?

5. Read Luke 6:43-45. What does the parable of the tree and its fruit mean to you? Can you give an example of how a person speaks "from the overflow of the heart"? In what ways can you make sure that the words you speak and your actions bring forth good and not evil?

"My high-school English teacher came back from teaching at a college to teach my senior class. I was editor of the annual and she was the sponsor. Later she retired and went to a nursing home. I went to see her during her last days there. There was a song out at the time about being irresistible; and she looked at me and said, 'Kay, you're not irresistible, but you're irrepressible. You're going to make your mark.' She chuckled and said, 'And that mark is going to be good.' I've realized that the words we speak to others can have such an impact. I've a lot of emails from people who I spoke to at a store or people who worked at an arena where we were playing a game, and they were now writing me telling me about it. Of course, I don't remember those because they were such short encounters. But they were writing and telling me about what kind of impact and impression I made on them going forward in life. In James 3, he talks so much about the power of the tongue. I think we just have to be so aware of that. I also know that in Philippians [2:3-4] we're told not to think more highly of ourselves than we ought to and to put others' interests ahead of your own. That's why I remind myself, *What am I doing today? What mark am I making today?*"

—Kay Yow

11

Laying It on the Line

Jon Kitna
NFL Quarterback

*Therefore, brothers, by the mercies of God, I urge you to
present your bodies as a living sacrifice, holy and pleasing to God;
this is your spiritual worship.*

ROMANS 12:1

Whatever you do, don't do it halfway.

BOB BEAMON

Mixing faith and athletics has always been a tricky proposition. Some believe the two are inseparable, while others don't think God has—or even cares to have—a place in the sports world.

In 2001, the folks at Catholic Supply decided to throw their opinion into the public arena by releasing a series of statuettes that depict Jesus playing various sports (baseball, golf, tennis, hockey, and so forth) with adolescents. These figurines quickly became a big hit but also took plenty of shots from the media and the entertainment world—in particular from Conan O'Brien, who regularly included them in innocuous comedy bits on his late-night talk show.

One of the most interesting pieces in the series shows Jesus—in a white robe and with sandals on his feet—playing football with two boys. As He hands the ball off to one young athlete, the other has Jesus wrapped up and ready to tackle. The depiction raised some interesting philosophical questions about Christ's nature—questions that NFL quarterback Jon Kitna has heard on numerous occasions.

"Some people say, 'How would Jesus play football? It's too violent a game. He wouldn't have played.'" Kitna says. "That's not true. Jesus would have been the most intense guy! He would have knocked people down, but then He would have helped them up and would have probably given them some Scripture along with it to encourage them."

While some may scoff at Kitna's assertion, he is emboldened by passages in the Bible that encourage believers to live with a paradoxical combination of singular focus and reckless abandon. "There's a right way and a wrong way to play the game," Kitna says. "You just try to play it the right way—within the rules, and within the biblical confines of how you're supposed to approach your craft. So as a quarterback, I think that's the best way to lead."

Perhaps that's why Kitna has never been accused of being soft because of his faith. "No, that's never happened to me," Kitna says. "I mean, I'm sure people might think that because Christians kind of get that stigma, I guess. But I think when people see me play, that's not one of the things that they say about me."

One of the things Kitna would like people to see is that he fulfills his role on the team by displaying a steadfast attitude of excellence that reflects the character of Christ. He strives to live out Jesus' words in John 12:32, where He tells His disciples, "If I am lifted up from the earth I will draw all [people] to Myself."

Christ goes on to explain that His followers must allow His light to live inside them: "While you have the light, believe in the light so that you may become sons of light" (v. 36). For Kitna, this means doing his best to be excellent during times of preparation and times of competition. The last thing he wants is for nonbelievers to see him as flaky and lacking in substance.

"You know, I think a lot of times as Christians we want to say, 'Well, God will handle it,'" Kitna says. "Yeah, God does make things happen. But He also relies on us to handle what we can handle. He gives us abilities, and we have to do what our job is here on earth. And He takes care of the circumstances we can't control. He takes care of those things. And so, for me as a quarterback, I mean, it would be nice for me to just say, 'Oh, I can just throw the ball anywhere, and if God wants it completed, He'll get it completed. If He didn't want it to be intercepted, it wouldn't get intercepted.' That's not reality. The reality is that I have a job to do. I have to do everything as if unto the Lord. I have to submit to the authorities placed above me. And those are all things that I try to incorporate into my life and in the way that I play football."

Kitna has also come to understand the unique relationship between adversity and excellence. It's a truth that is often hard to swallow but when embraced can bring amazing results in the long run. In 2 Corinthians 12:7-10, Paul used a moment of extreme transparency to teach the Early Church this very principle:

> To keep me from becoming conceited because of these surpassingly great revelations, there was given me a thorn in my flesh, a messenger of Satan, to torment me. Three times I pleaded with the Lord to take it away from me. But he said to me, "My grace is sufficient for you, for my power is made perfect in weakness." Therefore I will boast all the more gladly about my weaknesses, so that Christ's power may rest on me. That is why, for Christ's sake, I delight in weaknesses, in insults, in hardships, in persecutions, in difficulties. For when I am weak, then I am strong (*NIV*).

This Scripture was especially real to Kitna during the 2006 season, when his Detroit Lions suffered through an excruciating 3-13 season. "That season grounded us that year and grew our roots deeper," Kitna recalls. "I felt like it was a pruning process for us as a football team. And we had a lot of new Christians. And success can kind of be a bad thing for a new Christian, because then they just kind of tend to float. But when you don't have a lot of success, especially in this league, as a Christian you start to really learn what God's character really is and how much He really loves you. And then you become grounded and rooted. And then when you have the success that I think God is bringing our way, now we're already rooted. Now we're already solid. We have that solid foundation."

That experience also reminded Kitna of the truth found in 1 Peter 5:6-7: "Humble yourselves therefore under the mighty hand of God, so that He may exalt you in due time, casting all your care upon Him, because He cares about you."

Excellence also requires the ability to overcome any obstacles that stand in the way, not letting them slow the pace. Oftentimes, those roadblocks come in the form of doubters—people who intentionally or unintentionally distract us from that pursuit. Kitna, however, sees those individuals as opportunities for evangelism.

"You're always going to have those who don't believe—the skeptics," Kitna says. "But I say that [Satan] can try to use that all he wants, but really, that promotes great conversation. And that's growth. If we all believe the same thing in there, there would be no growth. But since there are varying levels of belief in the locker room, that promotes growth. It helps us have to learn about others' beliefs so that we're not blind to the fact that there are other beliefs out there. But then it also helps for us to have to know why we believe what we believe, so we can answer those questions."

Whether the pursuit for excellence is in athletics, academics or personal ministry, Kitna always comes back to the basics. As the early Christian author Lactantius once wrote, "God, who is the Eternal Mind, is undoubtedly of excellence, complete and perfect in every part." Therefore, following the example of His Son is undoubtedly the best way to achieve excellence and reach others in the process.

"The great thing is that if you do things as Christ did, all you've got to do is preach the Bible," Kitna says. "You don't have to argue with anybody. Just tell them what the Bible says. If they have a problem with it, then they have a problem with what the Bible says, not you."

Another key to obtaining excellence is honest assessment followed by a Spirit-led prioritization of everything in your life. Otherwise, distractions will get you off the narrow path, leaving you grasping at those proverbial straws. It's not always been an easy task for Kitna, but he can honestly say that the process has made all the difference in the world.

"You have to look at your life and look at yourself and ask, *What helps me be my best? What helps me stay focused on doing my best and doing my job to the best of my ability?*" Kitna says. "Anything that doesn't fit in that box, you can't visit those things. The enemy's always trying to distract us. He's coming to steal, kill and destroy. But we have to stay focused, so you have to know what fits in your box. For me, it's faith, family and then football. And if I get that order mixed up, it will always fall apart for me. If I put football before my faith or if I put football before my family, no matter how good of a football player I am, it's not worth it for me to lose my faith or to lose my family. It's not worth it."

Prioritizing everything in your life makes it much easier to stay focused on both the earthly goal of excellence as it pertains to bringing glory to God as well as the heavenly goal that is yet to come. As the apostle Paul writes in Philippians 3:14, "I pursue as my goal the prize promised by God's heavenly call in Christ Jesus."

"If I can just focus on my relationship with Christ, He takes care of all the other stuff," Kitna says. "He makes me such a better person that it takes care of my marriage, it takes care of my kids, it takes care of me as a football player in my job. But when I start focusing on my job, then I start to become less of a person in all those areas."

Kitna's intense pursuit of excellence also demands accountability from those who are closest to him. That starts at home with his wife, Jennifer. Kitna credits her for much of his success in life, thanks to her uncanny ability to keep him moving forward.

"My wife is a prayer warrior," Kitna says. "She loves Jesus. And she is just always on her knees praying for her husband. She knows the daily grind and the pressures and the scrutiny that you go through playing in this league. When I come home, she's always willing to let me just pour my heart out—if I've had a bad day or whatever it may be. But at the same time, she's one who will tell me, 'You're wrong in this situation. You should have done this differently.' And I always listen to her very closely, because I had somebody mentor me one time say that our wife is like the Holy Spirit for us. And they have a way of being intuitively in tune with situations that not everybody can see."

Another teammate in Kitna's spiritual journey is Lions' team chaplain Dave Wilson. During the 2007 season, for instance, Kitna met with Wilson every Saturday night for a time of discipleship. He experienced great growth throughout that year, which strengthened him as he pushed ahead toward excellence.

141

"There are some things that as the quarterback of a football team you go through," Kitna explains. "The enemy is real and the spiritual battle is real. So Dave would help me work through those things. But he was just awesome in the way that he lays his life down all the time to serve guys in the locker room. He's a model servant on the road. He goes on all our road trips. He's always helping out, picking up dirty laundry, picking up our tape and our garbage on the floor in the locker room and cleaning it up. He serves. He just has a great amount of love. He's standing on the sideline. He's praying all the time. He's praying for the team. He's just interceding all the time."

So many athletes today find themselves doing the exact opposite of what Kitna has embraced. They run from accountability and try to rely on their own strength. As far as Kitna is concerned, however, excellence on those terms is nearly impossible.

"That's why Dave Wilson is huge," he says. "That's why all my teammates are so important. We encourage each other. One time I was encouraging another player to get into the Word and into prayer every day; and he was like, 'I haven't been able to get in that.' And my question to him was, 'Would you come out onto the football field without your helmet on?' He answered, 'No, of course I wouldn't.' And I replied, 'Well, why would you go into life without praying, or go into your day without reading God's Word?' That's like not putting on your armor. That's like not putting on your helmet. You're going to lose."

Kitna is part of a core group of players who text each other every day with Scriptures and prayer requests. They also convene for what he calls covenant conference calls every couple of weeks, during which they ask each other brutal accountability questions. This is yet another part of Kitna's path to excellence.

"We try to hold each other accountable," he says. "That's the biggest thing, asking all these accountability questions. That's the way to do it. If you try to do it on your own, you'll lose every time—every single time."

Kitna hates to lose on the field. But he also understands that losing off the field in the game of life has eternal ramifications and requires a much greater level of purposeful intensity. It is that understanding that drives him to adhere to the mindset of Paul, who wrote these words in 2 Timothy 4:6-8 not long before he was martyred for the sake of Christ's Gospel:

> For I am already being poured out as a drink offering, and the time for my departure is close. I have fought the good fight, I have finished the race, I have kept the faith. In the future, there is reserved for me the crown of righteousness, which the Lord, the righteous Judge, will give me on that day, and not only to me, but to all those who have loved His appearing.

Paul's words make clear why excellence to Kitna is wrapped up in his unquenchable desire to be like Christ and is never defined by any temporary glory the NFL can offer. "The most important thing," Kitna says, "is to live my life with Christ set apart as Lord of my life."

TRAINING TIME

1. What kind of sports or games do you think Jesus would have played when He was a boy? What kind of competitor do you think He would have been?

2. Read John 12:32-36. What do you think Jesus meant when He told His disciples, "If I am lifted up from the earth I will draw all [people] to Myself"? What does being "sons of light" have to do with living a life of excellence? How can applying that to athletics or other areas of your life impact others?

3. Read 2 Corinthians 12:7-10. What are some possible explanations for the thorn in the flesh that Paul talks about in this passage? Can you share a weakness that you consistently have been faced with in your pursuit of excellence?

4. Read 1 Peter 5:6-7. Why do you think humility is required before God can "exalt you in due time"? What are some ways that you have been humbled in your life? Can you describe a time when an embarrassing situation gave you the opportunity to share Christ?

5. As a football player, Jon Kitna lays it all on the line. He says this requires spiritual accountability. Who are some people you rely on for accountability as an athlete? As a Christian? How does that accountability help you give your all on and off the field?

"In 2006 we were 3-13, and it couldn't have been a worse year in terms of wins and losses. At the end of the season, I spent a lot of time in prayer and looking back. Yeah, we want to win. I want to win. I want to do everything my coaches ask me for, but ultimately who am I playing for? And that's for Christ. So when things were at their bleakest, when things were just not looking good at all, and it seemed like a no-win situation, did I still come to work like I had a chance to win the Super Bowl? Did I still come to work and play with that kind of intensity? And can I look at myself in the mirror and say I did everything as if unto the Lord? Well, if that's the case, then God is saying, 'Well done, good and faithful servant.' We were 3-13, but there were guys getting saved. There were marriages being reconciled. We had 18 different people get baptized, between players and their spouses. We had a couples' study that averaged about 30 people coming week in and week out. So while the wins and losses were very disappointing, I don't think that God looked at last year as a disappointment for this football team, because people's lives were changed. And people's names were written in the Book [of Life] for the first time ever. That's always going to override any wins and losses."

—Jon Kitna

12

Redefining Success

John Wooden
Former UCLA Head Men's Basketball Coach

---

*Therefore, my dear brothers, be steadfast, immovable, always excelling
in the Lord's work, knowing that your labor in the Lord is not in vain.*

1 Corinthians 15:58

Losing is no disgrace if you've given your best.

Jim Palmer

When people think of excellence in higher education, Oxford University is often mentioned. That's because some of the world's most foundational philosophical ideas in government, religion, sociology, literature and business have been intellectually designed and developed by men and women who attended its various colleges. Luminaries such as John Wycliffe, Adam Smith, John Wesley, William Penn, J. R. R. Tolkien, T. S. Eliot, Margaret Thatcher and C. S. Lewis are just a few notables to have walked Oxford's hallowed halls.

But anyone who believes brilliance can only come from places like Oxford, Cambridge or perhaps places in

America like MIT or the Ivy League schools fails to recognize the simplicity of wisdom.

For legendary UCLA Bruins basketball coach John
Wooden, everything he truly needed to know about life
didn't take place in college—although he did quite well
while attending Purdue University—but instead was
taught to him and his brothers by Joshua Wooden on a
farm in Centeron, Indiana.

Wooden's father ingrained two key principles into his
heart and mind that became the cornerstone of a successful coaching career and that have, in turn, impacted
the lives of countless athletes and fans: (1) Don't try to be
better than someone else, and (2) always try to be the best
you can be.

"Dad reasoned that whether we were better than
someone else should not be the focus because our position in relation to others was out of our control,"
Wooden explains. "We could not control another's performance, nor could we control how we would be ranked.
All we could do was our best. . . . He wanted us to try very
hard to give the best possible effort to become the best we
could be and let the results take care of themselves."

Wooden took his farm-boy sensibilities with him to
Purdue, where he played basketball, and then to the high-
school coaching ranks, where he was increasingly dissat-
isfied with the educational system's definition of success.
By 1934, he had devised his own personal definition that
has since become synonymous with excellence.

"Success is peace of mind that is the direct result of self-satisfaction in knowing you did your best to become the best that you are capable of becoming," Wooden says. "Within this framework, each person becomes the only one who can ultimately judge his or her own success."

For Wooden, excellence breeds success, but both of those terms should be determined by effort and not necessarily the end result. His philosophy is quite different from today's model of success, which is generally measured in wins and losses—he contends that true success comes from the heart.

Enthusiasm, for instance, is one of Wooden's essential keys to excellence. He believes that people must truly enjoy what they do if they are to succeed, and he points to Romans 12:11 for his biblical impetus: "Do not lack diligence; be fervent in spirit; serve the Lord." "If we don't enjoy what we do, we won't be able to push as hard as we need to push for as long as we need to push to achieve our best," Wooden says. "However, if we do enjoy what we do and if we're enthusiastic about it, we'll do it better and come closer to becoming the best we can be."

Another important cog in Wooden's wheel of success is what he refers to as industriousness. He experienced the vital nature of hard work firsthand on the farm where his diligent parents led by example. Wooden says that's how a disciplined work ethic became part of his nature.

"There is no substitute for hard work," Wooden says. "Most people have a tendency to look for shortcuts or at least for the easiest way to complete any given task. If we only put out a minimum effort, we might get by in some situations, but in the long run, we won't fully develop the talents that lie within us."

This proved true for Wooden as an athlete and as a coach, and it continues to be the case as he approaches his one-hundredth birthday.

"As a basketball player, I wanted to be in the best possible physical condition," he says. "There was a time when I'd tell myself, *I'm going to be in better condition than anyone else.* As I grew older, my thinking changed to, *I'm going to be in the best possible condition I can be.* I had learned that I only have control over myself."

By exercising this principle, Wooden has reaped the benefit of Proverbs 21:5: "The plans of the diligent certainly lead to profit, but anyone who is reckless only becomes poor."

Wooden's profit as a basketball player included a national championship at Purdue in 1932. In 29 years as a college coach (including two seasons at Indiana State), he led UCLA to 10 NCAA championships. His team's enthusiasm and hard work (among other foundational values) led to competitive greatness—although he is quick to point out that winning should never be used as a barometer of excellence or success.

"Having competitive greatness does not always mean that you are the one who scores the most points or hits the winning shot," Wooden says. "Lewis Alcindor [now

Kareem Abdul-Jabbar] could have set every college scoring record in the book. However, he didn't. He could see the big picture, always reining in his own play for the sake of elevating the play of his teammates.

"We don't have to be superstars or win championships to reach competitive greatness," Wooden adds. "All we have to do is learn to rise to every occasion, give our best effort and make those around us better as we do it. It's not about winning. It's about learning to give all we have to give."

And that brings us back to Wooden's time-tested definition of success, in which winning is actually irrelevant. What's important is giving one's all. "We are the only ones who really know the truth about our own capabilities and performance," Wooden reemphasizes. "Did we do our best at this point in our life? Did we leave all we had to give on the field, in the classroom, at the office or in the trenches? If we did, then we are a success—at that stage of our life. But being successful at one point doesn't necessarily make us a success at every point—and it does not mean that we reach the apex."

Instead, success (the by-product of excellence) can be summed up in Jesus' parable of the talents found in Matthew 25:14-30. In that story, the ultimate reward for excellence came when the slave successfully took the money his master had given him responsibility over and increased its value. Verse 21 tells us, "His master said to him, 'Well done, good and faithful slave! You were faithful over a few things; I will put you in charge of many things. Enjoy your master's joy!" In other words, it's all about doing the most with what you are given that constitutes Christ-centered success.

"No one truly knows whether a person is excellent or has performed excellently, because what might be seen as excellent in the eyes of one might not be in the other's," Wooden says. "I feel that only the individual can really know whether they have executed near their level of competency. They must make the effort to execute near their own level and not be concerned about somebody else. Don't try to be better than they are. Try to be the very best you can be. And I don't care how good that is in the eyes of others'. To me, that's success. That's being excellent."

TRAINING TIME

1. In your sport or field of interest, how is success typically defined? How do you usually define success for yourself? Can you describe a time when you succeeded at something without giving your best? How did you feel about your success after the fact?

2. John Wooden's father used to tell him, "Don't try to be better than someone else." How does that philosophy differ from the idea of competitive success that most people have? What are some ways you could follow that advice while still striving for excellence in whatever you choose to do?

3. Read Romans 12:11. What are some ways that we can show enthusiasm in sports and in life? In what ways has enthusiasm helped you stay on track in your pursuit of excellence? What are some things that have at times challenged your enthusiasm?

4. Read Matthew 25:14-30. What are some things these talents represent in your life? What kind of personality and character did the first two servants display? How was the third servant different?

5. Who are some people who have excelled despite not having as much talent or natural physical ability as others? In what ways have you seen that philosophy ring true in your life?

"Fight is a determined effort to do the very best we can do. On the basketball court, fight is measured by hustle: diving to the floor for loose balls, sprinting to fill a lane on a fast break, taking a charge, picking up a missed defensive assignment or stealing the ball from an opposing player. It's digging in, gritting our teeth, standing our ground. When we have fight, we are always ready to respond. We are quick, but we don't hurry. We make fewer mistakes, because we have the level of our intensity under control. A player with fight has a contained fire burning in his or her belly. This emerges as focused passion. Players with fight never lose a game; they just run out of time. These days, I hear a lot of talk about getting up for a big game. No game should be any bigger than any other. People with fight can't get up any higher for an important game because they get up for every game. When people with fight step onto the floor, they always give everything they have to give, whether it's for a practice, a scrimmage or a championship game. There's no such thing as losing when we've made the effort to do the best we can do. If we use our fight and determination to do our best, success will take care of itself."

—John Wooden

THANKS

Fellowship of Christian Athletes would like to give honor and glory to our Lord and Savior Jesus Christ for the opportunities we have been given to impact so many lives and for everyone who has come alongside us in this ministry.

The four core values are at the heart of what we do and teach. Many people have helped make this series of books on these values a reality. We extend a huge thanks to Chad Bonham for his many hours of hard work in interviewing, writing, compiling and editing. These books would not have been possible without him. Thanks also to Chad's wife, Amy, and his two young sons, Lance and Cole.

We also want to thank the following people and groups for their vital contributions: Les Steckel, Tony Dungy, Jackie Cook, the Indianapolis Colts, Shaun Alexander, Todd Gowin, John Wooden, Chris and Tracy Byrd, Chris Klein, Kyle Petty, Richard Petty, Davis Hovis, Susan L. Williams, Petty Enterprises, Ryan Hall, Chris Anderson, Albert Pujols, Rick Horton, Melody Yount, the St. Louis Cardinals, Todd Perry, Kay Yow, Felicia Mangum, North Carolina State University Athletic Media Relations, Jean Driscoll, Jon Kitna, Tom Valente, the Detroit Lions, Chris Kaiser, Drew Dyck, *New Man* Magazine and Dave Bartlett.

Thanks to the entire FCA staff, who every day faithfully serve coaches and athletes. Thanks to our CEO and president, Les Steckel, for believing in this project. Thanks to the home office staff: Bethany Hermes, Tom Rogeberg, Dan Britton, Jill Ewert, Shea Vailes and Ken Williams. Thanks also to Bill Greig III, Bill Schultz, Steven Lawson, Mark Weising, Aly Hawkins and everyone at Regal Books.

Impacting the World for Christ Through Sports

FELLOWSHIP OF CHRISTIAN ATHLETES

Since 1954, the Fellowship of Christian Athletes has challenged athletes and coaches to impact the world for Jesus Christ. FCA is cultivating Christian principles in local communities nationwide by encouraging, equipping, and empowering others to serve as examples and make a difference. Reaching more than 2 million people annually on the professional, college, high school, junior high and youth levels, FCA has grown into the largest sports ministry in the world. Through FCA's Four Cs of Ministry—coaches, campus, camps, and community—and the shared passion for athletics and faith, lives are changed for current and future generations.

Fellowship of Christian Athletes

8701 Leeds Road • Kansas City, MO 64129

www. fca.org • fca@fca.org • 1-800-289-0909

COMPETITORS FOR CHRIST

Fellowship of Christian Athletes Competitor's Creed

I am a Christian first and last.
I am created in the likeness of God Almighty to bring Him glory.
I am a member of Team Jesus Christ.
I wear the colors of the cross.

I am a Competitor now and forever.
I am made to strive, to strain, to stretch and to succeed in the arena of competition.
I am a Christian Competitor and as such, I face my challenger with the face of Christ.

I do not trust in myself.
I do not boast in my abilities or believe in my own strength.
I rely solely on the power of God.
I compete for the pleasure of my Heavenly Father, the honor
of Christ and the reputation of the Holy Spirit.

My attitude on and off the field is above reproach—my conduct beyond criticism.
Whether I am preparing, practicing or playing,
I submit to God's authority and those He has put over me.
I respect my coaches, officials, teammates, and competitors out of respect for the Lord.

My body is the temple of Jesus Christ.
I protect it from within and without.
Nothing enters my body that does not honor the Living God.
My sweat is an offering to my Master. My soreness is a sacrifice to my Savior.

I give my all—all the time.
I do not give up. I do not give in. I do not give out.
I am the Lord's warrior—a competitor by conviction and a disciple of determination.
I am confident beyond reason because my confidence lies in Christ.
The results of my effort must result in His glory.

Let the competition begin.
Let the glory be God's.

Sign the Creed • Go to www.fca.org

Fellowship of Christian Athletes Coach's Mandate

Pray as though nothing of eternal value is going
to happen in my athletes' lives unless God does it.

Prepare each practice and game as giving "my utmost for His highest."

Seek not to be served by my athletes for personal gain, but seek
to serve them as Christ served the church.

Be satisfied not with producing a good record, but with producing good athletes.

Attend carefully to my private and public walk with God, knowing that the
athlete will never rise to a standard higher than that being lived by the coach.

Exalt Christ in my coaching, trusting the Lord will then draw athletes to Himself.

Desire to have a growing hunger for God's Word, for personal
obedience, for fruit of the spirit and for saltiness in competition.

Depend solely upon God for transformation—one athlete at a time.

Preach Christ's word in a Christ-like demeanor, on and off the field of competition.

Recognize that it is impossible to bring glory to both myself
and Christ at the same time.

Allow my coaching to exude the fruit of the Spirit,
thus producing Christ-like athletes.

Trust God to produce in my athletes His chosen purposes,
regardless of whether the wins are readily visible.

Coach with humble gratitude, as one privileged to be God's coach.

FELLOWSHIP OF
CHRISTIAN ATHLETES